THESE DOORS

MARIAN MATHEWS CLARK

Ames | Berlin | Lemgo

Culicidae Press, LLC
918 5th Street
Ames, IA 50010
USA
culicidaepress.com
editor@culicidaepress.com

Ames | Berlin | Lemgo

ISBN-13:   978-1-68315-022-0

Cover design and interior layout © 2020 by polytekton
Original design of the diagram on pages 8-9 by Hayley Abbas
Original cover art of store image by Mel Vincent, 1976

Table of Contents

Acknowledgements

To my West Coast Cousins—Linda, Dan, Kim, Donna, Bob and David—and my friends in Oregon, Iowa, across the country and in England, a shout of gratitude for opening your homes, screened-in porches and lives to me. You've kept me afloat with your phone calls, texts and e-mails, your crossword puzzles, your limericks, your Cornwall calendars, your glass flowers, your books and art pieces that surround me and your letters and cards that I've saved through the years. You've reminisced with me about the 'old days,' sustained me with wonderful meals, traveled with me across land and sea, helped me find humor in trying situations, encouraged me to write despite all the rejections, and listened without judgment to my fears and dithering. I couldn't have survived the world and appreciated its surprises without you.

To Pat Stevens, Bart Yates, Jim McGreevey, Laraine Nelson, and my Iowa City Writing Group, thank you for critiquing my stories with sharp minds but never sharp tongues. To Julie Claus, thank you for promoting my COVID poem, even though I'm usually not a poet. To Alex Flowers, thank you for reminding me that I can only write my truth, that anything else is a sham.

And a very special thanks to cousins Bob Mathews and David Wright who, though they didn't live in the burg of *These Doors*, experienced life along with me in a burg every bit as quaint and remote as that one.

Thanks to tech savvy Hayley Abbas who drew the original family chart for the book and to Steve Kennevan who calms my 'computer hysteria' and installs Skype and WiFi and Zoom and whatever else comes up that I'm clueless about.

And finally, thanks to Mikesch Muecke whose notion that books are important along with his commitment to publishing, brought *These Doors* into existence.

Disclaimer

Previous Publications

2019 O'jai Film Festival finalist with co-writer Patricia Stevens for feature script *Timber*.

First Place in Oregon's 2018 International Film Awards in the Feature Screenplay Category for *Timber*.

'My Study on Stay-Puts' story in *Crossing Class: The Invisible Wall* anthology by Wising Up Press, 2018.

Sixty-Something and Flying Solo: A Retiree Sorts it Out in Iowa, memoir by Culicidae Press, Ames, IA 2013. (Revised version, 2015)

'Getting There,' *Daring To Repair* Anthology, Wising Up Press, December 2012

'Just in Case: Alone at Christmas,' *Wapsipinicon Almanac*, December 2011.

'Getting There,' *Persimmon Magazine*," Fall 2008.

'The Dress,' *Dutiful Daughters*, Anthology, Seal Press, 1999.

'Just for the Time Being,' *A Ghost at Heart's Edge: Stories and Poems of Adoption*. Anthology by North Atlantic Books, 1999.

'My Study on Stay-Puts,' *The Sun*, Fall 1992.

'Flossie's Kid,' *Cottonwood Magazine*, June 1991.

'Houseboats and Peacock Feathers,' *Poets and Critic*, Sept. 1990 as a result of the Iowa Art Council's first place Fiction Award.

Relationships

Julia Webster – Valley Store Owner
Bert – Julia's father-in-law
Georgiana – Julia's mother-in-law
(Richard – Julia's deceased husband)
Darla Tarbell - Store Clerk

Murry Tarbell – Retired Logger and
Carl's brother
Barda – Murry's sister
Carter – Murry's   brother
Mother Tarbell – stroke patient who's not cogent

Lanny Mullins – Ex-con
Janice – Lanny's 2nd   wife
(Paula – Lanny's 1st wife he killed)

Joe Mullins – Lanny's uncle who's
secretly seeing Lydia

Hank Hekula – Farmer
Maybelle – Hank's wife
Doris Martin – Hank's cousin

Leo Martin – Retired Logger and Local Poet
Doris Martin – Leo's critical but faithful wife
(Liz Martin – Leo's niece in California)

Francoise Tarbell – Valley School Teacher
Darla Tarbell – Francoise's daughter
(Roy Jenkins – first husband, killed in Pearl Harbor)
Carl Tarbell – Francoise's second husband; Darla's stepfather

Harriet Jenkins – Portland Transplant and Activist
Sim – Harriet's husband and Roy's brother
(Irene – Roy's and Sim's possessive mother)

Lydia Robbins —Valley Store Clerk and Artist
Hallie – Lydia's granddaughter
(Jacki – Hallie's mother and Lydia's daughter who's
thought to be in some dive in Alaska)

Preacher Arlyn
(Bethany – Arlyn's estranged wife)
Maybelle – Arlyn's cousin

Sage Parker – Hippie
Terrill Parker – Sage's husband
Stephen – Sage's son
Terra – Sage's daughter
Olivia – Sage's sister

Chet Andrews – Retired Mill Edger
Clarence – Chet's son
Jerry – Chet's grandson
Melvin Thompson – Chet's friend
Gerald – Chet's friend

Buffalos

Julia

1959

They still slip out sometimes. Like the morning I point to the dairy case and say to Darla Tarbell who we hired for the summer, "Put the oldest buffalos in the front."

She nods without looking at me, then reaches, like it's nothing, to the back of the case and pulls three quarts of two percent forward. Once in a while I catch her staring at me as if I'm senile. Then I resent her more than usual. I tell myself someday she'll be old and not able to think right. But no matter how I try to convince myself, I know not everyone's brain goes haywire, no matter how long they live.

At least there aren't as many as in the hospital. The first two weeks, whatever I asked for—fresh water or help to the bathroom—all I heard were 'buffalos' coming out of my mouth. Nurses shook their heads and said right in front of me, "You'd think she'd say Richard. The poor man didn't even make it to the hospital. But buffalos?"

I spent the last year wondering about that myself. There was only once I caught a glimpse of the awkward things, thundering past the car on a drive-through animal reserve in Southern Oregon. It was a trip with my father, a month after Mother died. I was ten. I sat close to him, smelling his Palmolive shaving cream and feeling his cardigan against my arm. He was miles away in the silence draped around him since the funeral.

When those buffalos came from nowhere, bellowing and kicking up grass and dust, I slid onto the floor and curled into a ball I wouldn't unroll from. "Come on up here, Julia," my father said. "You're all right now. Nothing's going to happen."

"Julia?" It's Darla, calling from the vegetable shelf. She raises a can of Del Monte Beets. "Do you know how much I'm supposed to mark on these? Bert left a price on all the boxes but this one." Bert's making more mistakes lately. My father-in-law, a retired Boeing man, is too old to be running a store. But who else could I turn to? On his first trip to the hospital after I came to and it sunk in about the accident, I asked him to manage the place until I could figure something out.

Darla carries the beets to the counter where I'm perched atop my stool that doubles as a walker, now that I'm wired and stapled. "I should have checked before he went to Mills Port," she says, frowning. She doesn't like to make mistakes, which impresses Bert. He calls her 'very conscientious.'

As I inspect the can's green and red wrapper, I wish I could say, "Bert told me they're thirty cents." But ever since Darla showed up, he consults with me less and less. "Check with Georgiana," I tell her, setting the can, clunk, onto the counter.

Darla hurries with the can to the back of the store where Georgiana's sorting mail in the post office. She's Richard's mother and someone even I wouldn't trade places with. A made-up wreck of a woman with fuchsia lips and two-inch heels, she didn't move from Seattle with Bert. But after a couple months, she started coming around for a week, then ten days at a time.

Sometimes when I'm scraping my stool across the floor and Georgiana's leaning on the counter, dangling her earrings and smiling that pink or orange lipstick onto her teeth, we seem like a freak show. At forty-one, I'm pushing a stool and living with Georgiana's husband while Georgiana—sixty-five if she's a day—taps around in spikes and bats her eyes like a prom queen.

Then there's seventeen-year-old Darla in plain jumpers and no make-up. Bert claims we need her. Maybe he's right. But it makes things harder, being around someone who has her whole life ahead of her and still doesn't know how things might turn out.

Even if you know, life can throw you for a loop. When Richard suggested we move to these woods from Portland, I said, "You can't be serious. To the middle of nowhere?"

"It's a real find," he said. "A seventy-year-old general merchandise store. Built before the turn of the century."

"That Valley's nothing but a low spot, socked in by firs," I told him.

But he was sold on the place and talked it up. "No smog," he said. "No traffic. And eventually your own book exchange." He grinned. "Besides, there's a poem over the door by the local poet saying, 'The best people in the world pass through these doors.'"

I laughed and reluctantly said I'd think it over. I loved walking to Liggorio's Deli around the corner from our apartment and browsing in the *New to You* bookstore. Before I was married, I saw a movie a week and kept a running list of my favorites.

But lying in our cramped quarters at night, listening to neighbors argue and the horns and sirens on the street that ran past our bedroom, I let myself imagine quiet nights in the country, long walks in the cool woods and, of course, frequent trips to the city. I finally agreed to a trial period. Who knew the verdict would come in too late.

At five-thirty, a half-hour before closing, things are quiet. The only regulars who haven't picked up their mail are the Mullins brothers who often come out of the woods after six. Murry Tarbell comes Mondays, Wednesdays and Saturdays. His sister Barda doesn't allow Tuesday, Thursday trips to the store, mail or no mail. And since Darla started working here, her mother Francoise hardly ever comes in. She's the local teacher and the only one who has acted interested in my book exchange. I kind of miss her.

I climb off my stool and push it ahead of me over the rough planks to the back of the store. The smells of cascara bark and nails and fuel oil drift from the storage room. I park the stool at the bottom of the handrail and begin pulling myself up the eleven steps. Bert installed the railing after the accident.

I coax myself along. Left foot up one step, pull with the arms, settle the right foot beside the left, not too close or they'll get tangled. The second step, the third. I rest a minute. My arms are my strongest parts.

Then four, five, six. Halfway, I smell Bert's pipe and Georgiana's perfume and cinnamon toast from breakfast. I feel sweat on my forehead.

The first time I climbed these stairs, I was anxious. What would I be moving into? But nothing could have prepared me. Especially for the bedroom, wrapped in wallpaper of ships on puce waters. And the kitchen's sunflower and poppy wallpaper hadn't seen sunny days for years, ever since soot from the old oil stove clouded the skies.

The floor creaked and groaned. I wondered when it would collapse and I would find myself stretched out below in the vegetable bin or draped over the cash register.

After the first week I told Richard, "I don't think I can stay here. It's too gloomy."

"Oh honey, you're just not used to things yet. We'll re-paper soon," he said, on his way to the desk to balance the day's receipts. But after seven years, we replaced the plumbing, the roof, and built a lunch counter. Who had money left to redecorate?

"I don't think Darla needs to work at the counter," I tell Bert at dinner. We're in the kitchen, now white as a snowstorm. Georgiana had it painted during her first visit. She said she couldn't eat in a room where it looked like a coal mine exploded.

"That buffalo's always hanging around the counter," I say.

Georgiana's dishing up dinner. When she's around, she cooks, something I can't make myself grateful for. Her food's like the walls—white and bland. Noodles and rice and unsalted potatoes. Bert makes meat loaf and lasagna.

He passes me a plate of soggy dumplings. "I can't do everything. I'm handing out mail in the post office and cooking burgers at the counter. When you go upstairs to rest, I need help."

"I'm taking fewer rests lately," I tell him, irritated he hasn't noticed. Some days the only time I leave the cash register is to go to the bathroom. I shake my head 'no' at Georgiana who passes me a plate piled with slices of white bread.

"Why don't you sell this dump?" she says, clanking the plate down.

I don't answer. I need more time. Where am I supposed to go? I glance at Bert who acts like he isn't listening. He takes another bite of potatoes. Georgiana puffs a sigh.

I tried to make Richard listen. Several years after we moved to the Valley, I told him I still missed the city. "Let's not sink any more money here until we decide what we're going to do. We could buy a place in Portland," I told him.

But he said nothing could have the charm of this country store. And he only had one more addition on his list: a lunch counter. It would be the only eating place in town and would pay off in no time. After that, we would build shelves for my book exchange. I saw how much he wanted to stay and silently vowed to give it one more year.

"The girl hovers," I tell Bert then point to the plate of bread. I'm not quite full but worry all that dough might keep me awake. I've always had a hard time sleeping, but since the accident I'm lucky to drift off before three. "She's always at my elbow."

"She's just trying to help," Georgiana says then clicks her tongue. "Drat. This nail's a mess. I chipped it on the meat case."

I hand her the emery board she points to on the counter. Her nail paraphernalia's in every room.

"She's a hard worker," Bert says. He sops up the last of the broth with his bread. He's gained twenty pounds since he moved to the Valley. He eats too fast and has high blood pressure. But he likes the store, especially when Georgiana's in Seattle.

I can see it's useless to talk about Darla, so I reach for my walker. Georgiana braces her foot against one side while I pull myself up and lean against it. Bert hooks a mug over the handle. Then I lift the walker forward and catch up to it, lift and catch up until I reach the veranda which stretches the front width of the store. It's bigger than my bedroom. On hot nights, Richard and I pulled our mattress out here to sleep. Sometimes we talked about flying to New York for vacation as soon as we had a few dollars ahead.

I slide open the glass door and lift my walker over the threshold. There's a gentle breeze, and the white sheets Georgiana hung out this morning flutter around my head. I duck low and thump along toward Richard's captain's chair near the front railing until I spot my bottle of gin by the chair. It's one of those rare days when gray clouds haven't blocked the sun, but now I see they're fringing the sky and creeping toward the Valley. It's not that Portland has more sun, just more distractions to help you forget the lack of it.

I drop into the chair, pour myself a mugful and take a slow, welcome sip. Below me, Highway 47, a gray conveyer, heads north and south out of town. I'm settling back in my chair when I see Preacher Arlyn drive by, heading home to an empty house. People say when he saw God, he got too religious and lost his family. I've never been religious and since the accident have a hard time believing God cares about us at all. But I feel kind of sorry for Arlyn. If you really did see God…well, I'm not sure what it might do to you.

I take another long sip. "All aboard. Hurry. All aboard," I say and toast the dusk that's starting to settle. Which way tonight? Sometimes I head past Darla's, toward the mountain's death road. But today I head South. I slip by the population sign—Timber 50—then glance back at the fence post signs that welcome you to town: "Clancy's whiskers tickled Nancy/ Nancy lowered the boom on Clancy/ Burma Shave."

Just past the old bridge where the Nehalem River slaps its pilings, I start to wind—zigzag, zigzag, speed up, slow down—mile after mile along the river. I hug my sweater to me against the shade from the wall of old growth crowding the road. Dark. Menacing.

Forty miles of zigging and zagging, speeding up, slowing down until finally, I glimpse headlights on the Sunset Highway heading to Portland. My shoulders relax as the umber trunks open onto alfalfa fields. And then I hold my breath and make a run for it. Faster, faster. Toward *The Nun's Story* at the Broadway or maybe...

"Julia?"

My heart leaps to my throat. Faster, faster.

"Julia? I'm talking to you."

"Yeah?"

"You'd better come in," Georgiana says. "You don't want to catch cold in this night air."

Kind of like saying, "Let's get that sliver out of your finger," after a tree has fallen on you. "Just a few more minutes," I tell her.

"Feeling pretty good are we? Well don't be long," she says and tap, tap, taps back inside.

I take deep breaths, feel my heart calm and sink into its cage. I swish my tongue around my mouth and whisper, "Bon Voyage," then raise my glass to the conveyer in the night.

July's hot this summer and Darla wears sandals and no nylons. She'll be a senior in September. She's more careful about rushing in behind the counter. Bert must have talked to her. Since the accident, taking care of the counter has been my job when I'm up to it.

Bert's training Darla to make burgers and shakes so she can run the lunch counter. He says, "She might as well learn all the ropes."

"I don't see why," I tell him. "She'll be going to college after this year." I was an English major, working in a bookstore when I met Richard. I read Sartre and Camus and liked Tennyson and

Wharton. I'd never dated and planned on finishing college and being an English teacher. But the day Richard walked up to me and whispered, "I'm looking for books on Management, but I'll buy anything you recommend," I was tongue-tied. He laughed and said, "Red's good on you," then asked directions to the business section.

After a year, we were married. I continued going to school part time and working in the bookstore. He teased me about swallowing books whole. He was a manager at Piggley Wiggley's but had his heart set on owning his own business. I suggested a book store, but he wanted to sell something with more to it. As if words aren't substantial.

"If Darla's leaving in a year, why try to teach her everything?" I tell Bert who's pulling a slab of bacon from the meat case.

"She'll probably work here next summer and maybe even the summers she's in college," he says. He turns on the bacon slicer, which whines a shrill whir.

"I'll bet she won't," I say, even though he can't hear me.

It's the last Friday of July and Darla's taking on more and more responsibilities. Customers act like she runs things.

At noon Leo Martin comes in. Bert's back in the post office. Leo nods hello to me then says to Darla, "Could you please get me a quart of propane?"

"Sure," she says and bolts toward the storage room.

"She's a good worker," Leo says. "Johnny on the spot."

"Yes. She's always buffalos." I wait a minute. "Around."

Leo opens the pop case, pulls out a six pack of cola and is on his way to the counter with his groceries when Darla returns with the propane. I'm waiting until he finishes gathering things before I step off my stool to write up his bill. My hip's hurting, and I'm saving my strength. But before I can stand, Darla darts behind the counter and pulls out Leo's tab from its slot.

"*I'll* write down the buffalos," I tell her.

"Oh, sorry. I thought you were tired," Darla says. She slips from behind the counter and starts unpacking the corn

United Grocers dropped off. Once all the cans are out of the box, she'll price them with the black marker I can't write evenly with anymore.

"That's all, Julia," Leo says. "I'm in kind of a hurry to get things sacked up. My crew is up Deep Creek, waiting for the oil and lunch." I know the girl's listening, ready to rush in. Why can't she mind her own business. I smile at Leo, a patient man—he's married to Doris, after all—and know he wouldn't say anything unless he had to.

I nod at Darla who walks quickly to the counter and takes the sack I hand her. She settles the pop and spam on the bottom, apples next and bread and chips on top, the way Bert taught her. And all the time she's carrying on a conversation. "How's Doris's flu?"

"I always worry with her heart trouble," Leo says. "But she seems on the mend. She insists we're going to the Centennial doings in Forest Grove this week-end no matter what. She told me, 'We won't be around for Oregon's next one.' The wagon train from Missouri's supposed to show up Saturday around noon."

"I hear President Truman gave them a send-off," Darla says. "Can you imagine traveling two thousand miles in a wagon?"

Richard had that same gift of gab—like his mother. I envied it at first, but over time, it seemed like a big show. I didn't mention it to Richard because he would have said he was just being friendly and how could you expect to run a business if you weren't nice. It wasn't being nice that I resented but acting like you cared more than you did.

When Leo leaves, Darla runs her finger across the shelf under the counter. She checks her finger, wipes it across her jumper, then picks up a dust rag.

She's lingering which makes me antsy. I pick up *Woman of the World*, a novel about a rich globe-trotting heiress who's really a spy. I haven't read my favorites since the accident. Wharton's lonely, Tennyson depressing.

Darla sprays her rag with Pledge, pulls the sacks from under the counter and stacks them on the floor. Then she smiles at me. "Is your novel good?"

I shrug. "It's okay."

She wipes her rag across the shelf. "Do you read a lot of..." She tips her head to look at the jacket. "Sarah Carter?"

"I like Wharton and Tennyson," I tell her.

"I do, too." Her voice is eager.

"A lot of death, though," I say and immediately regret it.

She stops dusting, leans toward me and lowers her voice, confidentially. "I haven't gone through that yet," she says. "Not directly anyway. I mean my real father died in Pearl Harbor, but that was before I was born."

I nod then go back to my book, but Darla stares at me, waiting. I'm not about to discuss life with a girl whose idea of worry is not knowing the price to mark on a can of beets.

"I think the bolts of material need to be straightened in the back room," I say.

"Oh. Oh well, okay," she says and shoves the sacks back under the counter. Then she lowers her head and walks away.

I try to continue reading but can't concentrate. I guess it's natural for her to be curious. She's not the type to mean any harm. "Thanks for dusting," I holler after her. But she disappears into the side room without answering just as Bert strolls out from the storage room. He's sprinkling sawdust and kerosene over the floor around the meat case. Then he starts sweeping the mixture with the wide broom.

I watch his long steady strokes. Before the accident, I swept every day. The sawdust and kerosene kept the dust from flying and I liked seeing those plain, rough boards turn shiny and dark even though the sheen lasted only a few minutes.

When Bert passes the side room, he stops and says to Darla, "I'm going over the mountain to Mills Port for groceries tomorrow. How do the canned goods look?"

"The pig's feet is gone and Leo just bought the last of the barbecue chips," Darla tells him. Her voice sounds uneasy, like she's embarrassed. I didn't mean to hurt her. But if you're going to survive in this world, you can't be too sensitive.

"Make a list of what we need, will you Darla?" Bert says, as he sweeps the pile of dirt toward the front.

About half an hour before closing, I'm getting ready to make my trek upstairs for the night when three men saunter in. I glance out the window and see their truck with a sign on the side: *Northwest Re-seeders*. Passing through. Drifters.

I hear a tap, tap, tap on the stairs and Georgiana appears from the hallway, then stops and makes a beeline for the post office when she sees the men. I know she's preening, smearing on a fresh coat of lipstick from a tube she stashes in the dead letter box. Sure enough, when she reappears, her lips are a raging red. Tap, tap, tap, she makes her way to the whole-wheat and garlic bread. "I'll bet you boys have been slaving away all day. Where you working?" she says, moseying toward the front.

"Deep Creek," the oldest man says and starts making small talk about how the rain helped the seedlings but turned the ground so muddy, it was hard tramping around.

I look from Georgiana's catch to the youngest of the three who's inspecting the place, glancing into the side room, checking the post office. Then he asks Bert, "Where you keep the beer?"

Bert points to the liquor case, and then the kid flashes a big grin at Darla who blushes. She might be smart, but she doesn't know a thing about men. As green as I was at her age.

The third guy's poking around the packages in the meat case. But he keeps his eye on the young guy and Darla. Something isn't right. When he plunks his steaks on the counter, he asks Bert, "You have a gas can for sale?"

"I think there's an extra one out in the shed. I'll get it," Bert says and starts for the door. The steak man glances at the older guy, still talking with Georgiana, then walks to the back of the store.

They're spreading out. I try to stand, but my hip with the pin won't let me. Sometimes it doesn't work right. Finally, I'm able to rise a little, so steady myself halfway up by holding onto the cash register. The kid asks Darla how long she's worked here.

"Bert, I need some buffalos," I say.

"Stay there. I'll help you when I get back," he says.

I don't like the kid standing so close to Darla who's still blushing.

"Darla. Come here," I tell her, and see the kid squint at me when buffalos spill out. I yell, "Darla." Only buffalos.

They're so loud that Bert comes back. "What's wrong?" he says, irritated.

Georgiana says to the man whose ear she's bending, "She's been in a wreck. Says strange things sometimes."

"You can't trust them," I warn. But buffalos. Only buffalos. Last week I read in *The Oregonian* that small grocery stores are being robbed, and these guys are the type to do it.

"Settle down. I'll be right back," Bert says, then walks out, slamming the door.

"No, no," I scream. Just buffalos.

They're all looking at me now, and the men at each other, signals in their eyes. Darla takes hold of my arm. "Here Julia. You need help sitting?" She smiles, but her grip is firm. She doesn't see the danger.

Like Richard, the night we drove back from Mills Port. I told him, "Let's wait till tomorrow. The radio predicts black ice tonight. That mountain is bad enough dry." A thousand foot drop and no guardrails.

"You're such a worrier. I'll be careful," he said.

For ten miles he crept along. At the top there was the glisten. A short skid. I heard myself scream. Then we were fishtailing and spinning, then floating. Finally we were bouncing. I don't remember landing. I by-passed the crash and went straight to emergency. Richard by-passed the whole thing.

I shake my head at Darla who's still trying to push me onto the stool. I have to make her listen. "Watch out," I yell but buffalos, buffalos, tumbling out in a rush. The kid's right behind her. He'll grab her any minute. "Watch out, Darla. Watch out." Buffalos. Buffalos. Running for their lives.

He inches toward the cash register, but Darla doesn't notice. He has a wide mouth and eyes set narrow on his chiseled face. I glare at him. He steps toward me to stop the buffalos. He knows he has to move fast. His wolf eyes are the steely green of cold glass.

I'm still screaming, I'm surprised how loud.

"I've never seen her this upset," Darla says. "I don't understand." She pats my arm. "Julia, you're all right."

If only my bellows keep the wolf at bay a little longer. He reaches into his pocket.

Darla's still patting my arm. The man by the door clears his throat. The one in the back moves toward Georgiana, still babbling like a magpie. They're closing in. They need to hurry, but they don't know what to do with me. Darla, gently at first, then more firmly, pushes me onto the stool.

And then the door bangs open and Joe Mullins booms out, "What's all that racket?" It's the sweetest sound. Joe's two-forty and six-four, a giant of a man. His brothers, John and Nathan, trail in behind him. "We heard bellowing," Joe says.

Georgiana flutters over. "Julia's got a bee in her bonnet," she whispers, loud enough for the whole Valley to hear.

"That true, Julia?" Joe says.

I nod and smile.

"Well, a roar's good for the soul every now and then," he says to me, then "Howdy," to Georgiana's re-seeder, who grunts.

"How you boys doing?" Joe glances around. "Where's Bert? As long as we're here, we might as well eat."

"I can fix whatever you want," Darla says, stepping up to the grill.

Richard was frying a burger the day I told him I was planning to move back to the city. I was wiping off the salt shakers. "I need a change," I told him. "At least for a while." It was the day before the accident.

"Now? When we're finally almost in the black?" he said, laying down the spatula.

"Life's flying past. I'll be forty in a few days," I said.

"I thought you'd been happier lately. As soon as we pay off the grill, we'll hire someone to fill in. Then we can take a vacation." He came around the counter and sat by me.

"It's always one more thing," I told him.

"But you know how much I love it here," he said.

"That's why I've stayed so long. But I need something more for me."

"People are friendly. They try to include you."

"I'm not interested in pinochle or Grange. What about book stores, movies, the theatre, travel? What about..."

"I know we haven't been out for a long time. Saturday night, we'll go to Mills Port. For a nice dinner," he said.

I didn't say anything.

"Please, honey. Just a little longer." He put his arm around me and pulled me close.

I shrugged, tired from it all. Mills Port was a burg.

"It's a date, then?" he said, but his voice wavered, like it had finally sunk in he couldn't keep the store and me, too.

It looks like we're out of danger but I still keep an eye on Georgiana's man, leaning against the pop machine, looking daggers at us all. He motions to his buddies and they saunter out, just as Bert comes in without a can. One of them mumbles, "Nah, but thanks anyway," when Bert says he might have one in the back room.

I'm quiet while Joe and his brothers eat their burgers and talk about putting up a spar and the re-seeding which they say should be finished the next day. Georgiana glowers at me. She's lost her chance to corner her man again.

When everyone's gone, Darla starts piling dishes in the sink. Bert shuffles to the cash register to count the day's receipts. While he punches the keys, he says, "What burr got under your saddle, Julia?"

I clear my throat. "They were going to rob us," I tell him. My words come easy.

"What?" He stops counting and looks at me.

"Good grief," Georgiana says. "What makes you say a crazy thing like that?"

Darla stops washing dishes, a soapy glass in her hand.

"Their eyes. They were signaling to each other." No buffalos.

"These guys have been around for a couple months," Bert says.

"That's right," Georgiana says. "If they were going to rob us, they would have done it before now."

"Their eyes were mean," I say.

"You've been reading too many dime novels," Bert says.

Darla keeps looking at me, frowns, then turns slowly back to the sink.

Bert starts counting. Ones, fives, tens. "Looks like a pretty good day," he says.

"The young one was going to take care of Darla, the old one, Georgiana. And the other one..."

"Julia, Julia," Georgiana says, tap, tapping toward the counter. Then she sneers at Bert, "Make a million today, did we?" Her lipstick's licked off. She leans on the counter, her wrinkles sagging around her mouth.

"I scared them off. I..."

"That's enough," Georgiana says. "I'm going up. You coming?"

I don't answer, but Darla looks up from the dishes.

Georgiana waits, her lips pursed.

"In a minute," I say. Still no buffalos. I must have yelled them all out.

"Well, I hope you've made all the racket you're going to for one day. I can't take any more of that." Georgiana scowls at me. "I'm going up, Bert. You coming?"

He growls, "I'm in the middle of counting. Seventy-eight, Seventy-nine, Eighty..."

"I'm going to Seattle in a few days," she snaps, turns and totters toward the stairs.

"Good," he mutters. "Eighty-one, eighty-two, eighty-three."

Darla's drying the last glass. I wonder if someday, she'll realize my buffalos saved her. It only takes one small mistake.

I push myself to my feet. "Good night, Darla."

"Night," she says, her back to me. She slides the glass onto the shelf.

"Eighty-four, eighty-five, eighty-six... Hm. Not too bad."

"I'm going upstairs now," I say to Bert, hesitate and look at him.

"Eighty-seven, eighty-eight, eighty-nine..."

Maybe he doesn't hear me. I say, louder this time, "I'm going up buffalos," then shake my head but smile a little at the stubborn old straggler as I scrape, scrape, scrape my way across the bare boards.

Chances Are

Francoise

1960

Thursday, May 12

Saying 'no' wasn't easy. It didn't help that she burst into the house and bubbled out, "I won the scholarship, Mom. Summer in Japan. Mt. Fuji, Kyoto." And bursting and bubbling isn't Darla. Then she flung her arms around me.

It caught me so off guard, I said, "That's great, honey," then got my bearings. "But this isn't the summer for it."

She gaped at me. I started to remind her that Bert expected her to work at the store, but she walked out mid-sentence. The last time she did that was in the fifth grade when I said if I found her reading Nancy Drew again instead of practicing the piano, she couldn't go across the road to the playground for a week.

I'm sure she'll come around. It's not that we never disagree, but she's usually reasonable.

Today—trouble at school. Things seemed routine when I crossed the road to the schoolyard this morning for playground duty. Gunner Cox, hanging by his knees from the monkey bars, twisted sideways and said, "Can you do this, Mrs. Tarbell?" Assured him I couldn't, then told him to climb down before he fell.

After he made a grumbly descent, I walked to the end of the field where first and second grade girls were gathering cones, sticks and rocks to mend living rooms and kitchens they've laid out among the fir's giant roots. With small animals and boys messing things up, there are constant repairs. I gathered a few cones and piled them near the living room. "It looks like you're getting things back in shape," I said to Gunner's little sister who scooped up my cones and pointed to paw prints. "A raccoon," she said.

As a kid, Darla practically lived under that tree. Once we spent an afternoon laying out a house. Now she'll live in a dorm at the U of Oregon. A good thing I have teaching. But still...

At 8:25, kids crowded around while I unwound the rope to ring the school bell. As always, Gunner said, "Can I pull it, Mrs. Tarbell?"

"May I," I said and started to hand it to him, then saw someone running down the highway toward us.

"It's Lanny Mullins," Gunner said. "He had to walk."

"From home? It's three miles." I held onto the rope.

"His dad's mad at him because he's a chicken wuss," Gunner said and laughed.

"No name calling. You know our rules." There's a rivalry between those two.

"That's what his dad calls him. Lanny's scared to shoot a deer," Gunner said. "His dad said, 'I shot Krauts and have a wuss for a son. How the hell you expect to defend yourself, kid?'"

Before I could scold him, he said, "I'm not cussing. That's what his dad says." Then he reminded me he'd shot a buck and wasn't a scaredy cat to do anything. Even go to war.

I told him if he didn't spend more time on his math, he wouldn't be going anywhere. I hate being hard on him but have to nip this in the bud.

Saturday May 14

Thank heavens for the weekend. I had a restless night and Darla's barely speaking to me.

Carl left at seven this morning to help his brothers Murry and Carter re-roof their gun shop. Carl asked me to go with him to visit Mother Tarbell and his sister Barda, but I said I had papers to grade. They'd quiz me about Darla, and I don't want to talk about her right now. Scholarship winners will come out in the paper next week, and by then, I hope we have things settled.

I wish I felt closer to Carl's family. But if I mentioned Darla's trip, Carter would launch into a tirade about "the God damned Japs who shot at me and why in Hell would Darla visit that damned place." Even if I said I'd told her she couldn't go, he'd chew on it forever. Poor Murry doesn't criticize, but living with those two, he hardly gets a word in edgewise.

It's true what they say that you marry a whole family. I learned that with Darla's father, Roy. His mother clung to him and fainted at his funeral. She's still cold toward me. If it weren't for Darla, I doubt she would speak to me. It's as if Roy's dying at Pearl Harbor were my fault.

Carl's family's suspicious of outsiders. Carl says they like me but aren't used to company. He says Carter was different before the war. All I can say is "Who wasn't?"

After breakfast, I did a large hand washing and baked three dozen peanut butter cookies to freeze for the summer bazaar. I just started grading math papers at the kitchen table when Darla sat down with a bowl of cereal. She wouldn't look at me.

So I said, "Honey, you know I'm really proud of you for that scholarship." Her eyes lit up. But before she listed other Japanese sites she's dying to visit, I told her, "With getting ready for college, you have too much to do this summer. You have your whole life to study abroad."

"Not with a scholarship," she said. "I've already filled out the passport application."

Then she frowned. "I'll talk to Bert about work. He said to let him know as soon as I made my plans. I'll tell him I can work those last two weeks in August before school starts, long hours if he wants me to." She stopped frowning.

"Extra hours *and* pack for college?" I shook my head. "That's too much."

She set her jaw and stacked her dishes.

I hated bringing up finances but she needs to see reason. "Carl and I want to help you with college," I said. "But your chipping in a full summer's wages was part of the deal."

She studied me a moment, then pursed her lips and carried her dishes to the sink.

"This is probably our last summer together. Let's not spoil it," I said.

"*I'm* not spoiling it," she said and walked out.

Just a week ago we were sorting her clothes, deciding what she could use for college and what she should get rid of. We came across a Dirndl skirt she made in home ec class but never wore. The gathers were bunched up on one side.

"You sure you want to get rid of that?" I said as she tossed it on the discard pile.

"It's my one 'B," she said. "I only took that class because you wanted me to. Give me history or English, but don't ever again sit me in front of a sewing machine." We both laughed.

Now, I'm the enemy. I went to her room, but she wasn't there. I glanced around at her things. The things she'll take to college in just three months.

I looked out the window at the school yard and spotted her atop the monkey bars. As a kid, she perched there when she was upset. I wanted to go across and make things better like I used to. But I didn't know what to say.

Sunday Afternoon, May 15

I couldn't force myself to grade math papers so decided to write in my diary. I ended up reading every May entry since Darla was born. In a '42 entry I'd written "I'm worried about poison gas. Emergency instructions were listed in the newspaper. After a Japanese sub near Santa Barbara shelled the Bankline Oil Field, it's hard not to be afraid. The West coast is a natural target. And Timber is only sixty miles inland."

On May 5th of '45, I wrote, "A Japanese balloon bomb killed six picnickers south of here near Bly. I dream about soldiers, crawling across beaches and killing us in the night. Today, bought more black cloth to cover the north window. It's small, but you never know."

Darla's too trusting. It's dangerous to go traipsing across the world. Two weeks ago the Soviets shot down a US plane and captured the pilot. Things happen. And war turns you wary. Every night for four years we draped windows on the off-chance that someone, groggy and stumbling to the kitchen for a glass of water, would flick on a light. Chances are one flicker wouldn't matter. Chances are. But we cut and draped just in case.

Monday May 16

Darla was aloof this morning before she left for school. When I told her, "Good luck at the awards assembly," she said, "Thanks" politely. I hugged her good-bye, but she stood like a board. I feel rotten, but have to stick to my guns. It's for her own good.

I watched from the window as she climbed onto the bus, grown up in her black skirt and beige blouse. I thought of her in junior high in her aqua skirt with kittens chasing each other around the border. When I asked if she didn't want a pink poodle skirt like other girls wore, she said, "I like cats." She's always had a mind of her own.

Lanny's dad made him walk to school again today. His face was flushed. When he slunk into the schoolyard, he ducked his head, then ran up the steps into the building. After I took roll, Gunner groaned when I announced "Ten minute quiet time," but Lanny stuffed his head down into his arms. Hiding. I know how he feels. That's what I wanted to do when Roy was killed.

It's a good thing I had teaching. And Darla. I couldn't have survived without her.

Wednesday May 18

Darla stayed late at school to practice her valedictory speech with her English teacher. I told Carl at dinner she was still mad at me for not letting her go to Japan but that I thought it was too much with everything this summer.

"What's this summer?" he said, and nodded toward the potatoes.

"She has to get ready for college. And Bert's counting on her at the store. It's a lot." I passed him the bowl.

"And you'd miss your annual Shakespeare trip to Ashland," he said, an edge to his voice.

"We always invite you. And that doesn't have anything to do with it. It's all the other things. Besides, she has her whole life to go abroad."

"Not with a scholarship."

"Are you two in cahoots?" I pointed to the rolls.

"It's just that you've pushed her to study and go to college and be something." He handed me the basket. "I'm surprised you'd want her to pass this up."

"She *is* going to college. But Japan is 6000 miles away."

"Is it the distance or the place?" he said, his voice gentle.

"It's the whole summer," I said, irritated, then buttered my roll.

We were quiet a few moments. "Nathan made Lanny walk to school again," I said. "I guess he's still mad over Lanny's not wanting to kill a deer. I may have to talk to him."

Carl shook his head. "I doubt you'll have much luck. He's always had a mean streak."

"Making Lanny walk three miles is extreme."

"We used to walk..."

"Things were different then," I said. I know I was impatient, but I couldn't hear one of his old hardship stories right then.

Thursday May 19

Last night I went to bed early. When I finally dropped off, I dreamed Japanese soldiers were slithering through our orchard, gaining on Roy. He called to me. I reached out the window and pulled him in. We grabbed each other and hugged for a long time. He smelled of cut grass, like he'd just mowed. I didn't let him go until he gasped, "We forgot to shut the window." I jerked awake.

In the dream he was wearing the blue and green flannel shirt I gave him one Christmas. He'd left it with me saying he couldn't hula in flannel. He said, "I'll think of you wearing that shirt in the garden." I wore that shirt through my pregnancy. It was roomy and warm. I was wearing it the first time I felt Darla kick.

I wore it to *Golden Boy* where hula dancers shimmied their way through the newsreel. When I returned from the movie that night, I wrote Roy that Darla was kicking, kicking and that my stomach was stretched so big, if he saw me, he wouldn't call me his petite Francoise. At the end I said, "P.S. If you watch those hula dancers, keep your eyes on the hands."

Friday May 20

Before school, I heard Gunner making bock bock chicken noises at Lanny. I told him, "If I see you picking on him again, no recess for a week." His eyes welled up. I know the little stinker needs building up. He'll probably have to repeat third grade. So I praised him for being a good helper when he erased the board. He brightened up. "Guess what, Mrs. Tarbell. It's Mama's birthday, and tonight Daddy's taking us all to Portland for a movie." He said he'd tell me all about it on Monday. It's hard to stay mad at that kid.

Tonight when Darla was setting the table, I said, "Do you want to go to Portland to the movie? *Let's Make Love* with Gene Kelly's playing at the Paramount."

"Really?" she said, interested for a moment.

"We haven't gone to a movie for a long time."

"But would Dad like it? It's not a Western."

"I mean just the two of us."

She hesitated. "I have finals tomorrow," she said and set a glass of water by Carl's plate.

"It was a spur of the moment idea," I told her. "How many do you have?"

"Three," she said, and opened the silverware drawer. I watched her wrap her fingers around the forks and knives. Those slender fingers are the last remnant of her piano lessons. I thought she would take to it, but it was such a fight to get her to practice, I finally let her quit.

Wednesday, May 25

I'm glad it's Wednesday. It's been a tough few days. When I left for Arlyn's for prayer service, Carl said, "Drive carefully. Watch for deer on the road." Every Wednesday night he says that, the only time he warns me about driving. Maybe he thinks I'm tired mid-week. Or maybe it's his way of discouraging me from going to Arlyn's.

I did creep along, as it was foggy. And firs lining the road made it worse. I was glad to see the light from Arlyn's wishing well. He built it so parishioners could find their way on dark nights. It's red cedar with a small pail hanging from the archway. Charming, but not everybody thinks so. Bert said, "A wishing well for a congregation of two?"

People blame Arlyn that his wife and kids left him. Things aren't always as simple as they seem. I know he loved Bethany and wanted them to stay. But after he found religion, she wasn't able to. All I know is he helped me survive Roy's death. He said, "Keep a daily diary of what you feel, then hand everything over to God. You have to have faith." He threw me a lifeline. When you're drowning, you need survival tips from someone who's had to use them.

Tonight, I was the only one at Arlyn's as usual. The only other person who comes is Mrs. Hekula once or twice a year when she can't make it over the mountain to her own church. I wonder if Arlyn gets discouraged with attendance. How could he not?

He started the service by asking if I had blessings or concerns. I said Darla won a scholarship to spend the summer in Japan and was angry she couldn't go.

He frowned. "Why can't she?"

"She needs to get ready for college, and Bert's counting on her to work this summer."

"Oh, that's too bad. Has she talked to him?"

"It's just that there's too much to do. She'd be home for only two weeks then leaving for good." I was surprised at the irritation in my voice.

Arlyn's face flushed. "Do you want me to pray for…" Then he stopped, like he wasn't sure what to say. Even Arlyn didn't understand.

"I need to use the bathroom," I said and got up before he could close his mouth. It hit me that in all these years, I'd never been in his bathroom. I daubed water on my face and stared into the mirror. There were dark circles under my eyes. My hair was still auburn, but only because of Clairol. I asked myself, "What's going on with you?" but my eyes started to tear up, so I looked for a towel and found a frayed one on the shower rod. The shaver on the sink reminded me this was a man's bathroom and that Arlyn's been alone for years. How did he survive when Bethany and the kids left?

When I returned, I said I was sorry for being upset. He said he hadn't been much help. Then he prayed God would be with Darla and Carl and me. Before I left, he said, "I know this is a difficult time, but God will comfort you. And remember, you have Carl."

I nodded but thought of Darla's room, empty. For a moment I couldn't breathe.

Friday May 27

Today an eruption at school. Before I rang the morning bell, I was encouraged things were improving. Lanny was playing tetherball, and Gunner and Bertie waited in line to challenge. Lanny gave the ball a final smack that wound it tight just as the bell rang. Gunner said, "Good game," then smiled at me. He wants my approval constantly, but maybe that's okay if it keeps him from teasing Lanny. I walked in with Gunner who grinned and stood tall.

Once inside, I started the first grade on math and the second on social studies, then called for the third-grade reading group to join me in a circle. Lanny was the last one to the group, and the only seat left was next to Gunner. Lanny hesitated, but plopped down. At Lanny's turn to read, Gunner snorted when he said 'throwg' for 'through.'

I said, "None of that." Lanny glared at Gunner who mumbled, "Sorry," and Lanny seemed okay. He's been in a slinking mode lately but when the group finished, he walked upright to his desk.

Then it happened. During the bathroom break, a wide-eyed Bertie charged into the room.

"Fight in the bathroom," he said. "Gunner's got a bloody nose."

By the time I got there, a couple fourth graders had pulled Lanny and Gunner apart.

Lanny was straining to get at Gunner. Gunner was holding his puffy eye. While I was wiping his bloody nose, he blubbered, "I didn't do anything this time, Mrs. Tarbell. I was just peeing, and all I said was, 'Your dad's mean for making you walk to school.'"

Bertie nodded so hard, I thought his head would fly off. Lanny said, "Nobody talks about my dad," then glared at the floor. I kept him after school and tried to talk to him, but he was shut down. Something has to be done.

Saturday May 28

I woke early and made more cookies, then paid bills and cleaned the hall closet. When I walked into the den, Darla was ironing. "I don't know what I'll do without my ironer next year," I said. "I haven't had to iron since you were ten."

"Nine," she said, pulling Carl's work shirt from the basket.

"I can finish this if you need to study."

"I'm almost done," she said, draping the yoke over the end of the board. As I passed the desk, I saw her photo.

"What's this?" .

"My passport picture. I had it taken when I filled out the papers."

I studied it a moment and saw she has Carl's half mouth grin, as if she's holding off a real smile. Though Carl's not her father, at times she seems more like his daughter than mine.

"It makes me look cross-eyed," she said.

"You just look a little tired," I told her. "That's why this summer you need…"

"Mom, let's not talk about that. It just makes me angry."

"You're usually so reasonable about things."

She set the iron on the end of the board with a clunk. "Who's being unreasonable?" she said, her eyes snapping. "*You're* the one who wanted me to do well in school. And now *you're* the one who doesn't want me to accept a scholarship. It's been my dream to study cultures and religion, and this is the perfect chance. Mr. Hawkins says the family I'm staying with is…."

"We were at war with them."

"That's what I thought. We could get everything done in a couple weeks. You don't want me to go because it's Japan."

"We bombed Hiroshima. Do you really think they'll welcome you with open arms?"

"That was a long time ago." She straightened the sleeve of Carl's work shirt with a yank.

"Only fifteen years? Not nearly enough time to forget." I sat on the couch and motioned for her to sit beside me. "I want to tell you something."

"I can listen from here," she said, ironing the second sleeve.

I took a deep breath. "I never told you, but in your father's last letter, he said that when he'd told an old Japanese taxi driver in Hawaii the war was winding down, he laughed."

She looked at me a moment, then handed me Carl's shirt which I draped over the couch.

"It's true," I said. "The old man shook his head and repeated, 'winding down,' then laughed. "That was two days before the attack. He knew what was coming."

She picked up the last piece in the basket, my blouse, and shook it out. "Maybe he didn't know what 'winding down' meant."

"Don't be naive," I said. "When your father told him I was pregnant and showed him a picture of me, he stopped laughing. And at the end of the ride, he said he wouldn't take a tip. He said, 'No tip; no tip.' So your dad wrote, 'I'll buy something for the baby.'"

"That tiny orange and yellow shell Lei you gave me for my sixth birthday?"

I nodded, glad she remembered. I was making headway.

"I can't believe something that fragile made it from Hawaii."

"The point is that while Japan was making gestures to sign a treaty, they were planning an attack. Some people knew. All that hurt doesn't die easily—on either side."

She turned the blouse over and started on the other sleeve. "That's why it's important to try to mend old wounds," she said. "So we won't have another war."

"You trust too easily" I gathered up the ironed shirts and slacks and blouses. "Remember the incident with the old man?"

"Mom, I was ten."

"Well, last summer you said Julia was addled, thinking those men were planning to rob the store. But it turns out she was right. They robbed a store in Pendleton. When you get older, honey, you'll understand you can't trust everybody." Then I left the room.

As I walked down the hallway, I heard her mutter, "I hope I never get that old."

I went right to the phone and set up a meeting with Lanny's father. I need to straighten out that situation before Monday morning.

Sunday May 29

After a week of gray skies, we finally saw the sun. I planted pansies and impatiens, then bathed and drove to Arlyn's. His sermon was "Christ's unconditional love." His challenge for me, as I was the only one there, was to feel that way for everyone. It's something to aim for, but I doubt it's possible. The only person I love in that way is Darla. I love Carl, of course, but it's different.

After church, I stopped at Lanny's house for my meeting. Nathan answered the door. He invited me in with a friendly tone, pointed me to a brown couch with a very large brown and white doily on the back, then sat in a tan overstuffed chair with doilies on the back and arms. It reminded me of what I call Doily Heaven—Roy's mother's place. I expected Nathan's to have a spartan look. I guess harshly strict doesn't have to mean aesthetically spare.

I heard noises from another room, but Mrs. Mullins didn't appear. Maybe she was making doilies. When Lanny peeked around the doorjamb, I said hello, but Nathan shook his head and said, "Son, your teacher and I need to talk in private." His tone was kind and his calm attitude made me hopeful.

When I said I was concerned about Lanny's being withdrawn and angry lately, Nathan said he hadn't noticed anything. Then I told him he'd gotten into a fight Friday, unusual for him.

Nathan actually smiled and nodded. "He told me that," he said. "Glad to see the kid's finally showing some spunk. Can't lay down and play dead."

"It's not just the fighting but his attitude. He's changed from a happy kid to an angry one." I smoothed the doily. "It started when he had to walk to school."

"I'm just toughening him up," he said. "Getting him ready."

"For what, Mr. Mullins? He's in the third grade."

He sat forward in his chair. "You have a girl, Mrs. Tarbell. Ever raise a boy?"

"No, but…"

"If he goes to war, chickens don't make it. The reason I'm sitting in front of you now is because of what I learned, hunting these woods. A boy can't be afraid if he's gonna survive."

"Just because he won't shoot a deer, doesn't mean he's a coward. And even in war, not everyone fights."

He squinted, and I saw the meanness Carl talked about. "*My* boy would fight," he said. "*My* boy will be the first to join up. Now that Castro's in cahoots with the Russians, someone's going have to fight the Commies. You know you can't trust them. They're as bad as the Krauts, trying to take over the world. And *my* boy will be ready. I'll see to that."

"Mr. Mullins," I said, leaning forward in my chair and meeting his glare. "He's only nine. I can't sit back and watch one of my kids…"

"He ain't *your* kid," Nathan said, standing.

I rose, too. "As his teacher, I think of him that way. All I'm asking is for you to find a milder way to punish him. Maybe have him pack in wood or weed the garden. Something that doesn't make him a target of ridicule with the other kids."

I followed him to the door, but when he opened it, I stayed put. "He's not a criminal," I said. "Your punishment doesn't fit the crime."

He turned toward me. "You don't have any idea what it's like. The crime, as you call it, is hesitating a split second. I saw men die because, for just a moment, they hesitated to shoot a Kraut. A lousy Kraut." His eyes flashed. "I love my boy, but he's too soft-hearted for his own good, and I'll raise him how I see fit."

I stepped out onto the porch and said hurriedly, before he could shut the door, "You can't make him be who he isn't, Mr. Mullins, no matter how hard you try."

At dinner I told Carl and Darla about my talk with Nathan. "It's obvious how much Lanny wants his approval," I said. "Right now, he's scared to stand up to him. If Lanny was eavesdropping, he'll know somebody's on his side, even if he still has to walk to school."

"I have to hand it to you," Carl said. "I'm surprised Nathan didn't cuss you out."

Darla looked pensive, taking it all in. After dinner she went to her room to study.

As I washed the frying pan, I heard her behind me. "I thought you were studying," I said.

"I have to talk to you. It's what you said about Lanny's being afraid of his dad. It made me think why I'm afraid of you," she said, calmly.

"Of me?"

"I want to go to Japan."

My heart sank. "Sometime, just not this summer," I said. "The decision's made."

"That's what I'm talking about," she said. "I'm eighteen. I could just go. Except I've been afraid you would be upset. But like you said, we have to be who we are."

"I didn't mean follow every whim," I said, letting the pan sink into the greasy water.

She shook her head. "It's not a whim," she said, an edge to her voice. "I need to learn about people and their beliefs. That's who I am. That's what I *have* to do."

"You have your whole life." My voice was pleading. I cleared my throat.

"And this is the next part of it. I've decided to work this fall to help with tuition, then start school in the Spring. To keep my end of the bargain," she said, her voice firm.

"Carl and I won't let you do that. You're going to start..."

"That's my only option. You know if it were England, you wouldn't care."

I took a deep breath. "I admit it would make it easier," I said. "But...well...if you go... it's just that we don't have much time left together."

She looked surprised. "Mom, is that the problem? It's not like we won't see each other. I'll be home for holidays. And U of O is only four hours away."

I felt numb. She was ready to go. She reached to give me a hug, but I shook my head and turned toward the door.

"It's nothing against you, Mom," she said.

I nodded and left the room. She was right in some ways, which made me angrier. I needed time. I went to my bedroom and picked up my diary. Then I walked to the front of the house, crossed the road to the schoolyard and made my way to the old fir where I sat among the roots.

I would write it down, get it all out, then try to give it to God, as Arlyn suggested. I couldn't let her leave without being able to give her a genuine hug back. The sun was setting and I knew it might take a long time. So I brushed aside the cones and rocks that were poking me, and settled myself back against the tree.

In twelve hours, my first and second graders would be staring at these scattered cones, wondering what animal or pesky boys ruined their village. And no one would suspect it was me.

Lily of the Valley

Murry

1969

"Hurry Murry. Hurry Murry," my sister Barda bellows. "It'll be too late."

"Coming," I yell, then whisper, "I'll see you soon. Yes I will," to Miss Harper before closing the lid on her. I lock the dresser drawer and make my way to the staircase, grab the railing and inch myself down the narrow steps.

"Hurry Murry," Barda roars again. "I mean it." She always means it.

"I'm coming," I say, taking the last step. Ever since my accident in '29, my leg doesn't bend so well. And now, arthritis is setting in.

In the living room, Barda hovers over Mother's hospital bed. "What's so fascinating in your room that you have to see it during the day?" she says.

"Nothing." I think of Miss Harper's engagement picture with her hair curling around her nursing cap. After my Harley accident, I made the mistake of mentioning her. My brother Carter started mimicking me: "Miss Harper took my temperature. Miss Harper put her hand on my forehead. Miss Harper this, Miss Harper that." That was the end of telling. Yes it was.

"Murry's here, Mother," I say. "Murry's here." She's whimpering.

"I hope it's not too late," Barda says.

"She's been hollering for ten minutes," Carter says from his desk where he's twirled his chair around to stare at me.

"I came as soon as I heard you."

He spins back around to write in his weather diary and mutters this is the worst dry spell since '55.

I lift up the armload of yellow nightgown swallowing Mother. She's dropped to eighty pounds but for somebody like me, only a hundred forty myself, she's a load.

"Murry's here. We'll be in the bathroom in a jiffy." I lug her out of the living room and into the kitchen, narrower now with the stacks of newspapers and magazines. Barda's doing her spring cleaning which puts her behind on overalls and flannel shirts piled on the ironing board. I've told her, "Why iron those? We wear them in the woods. Who cares how loggers look?" But she can't stand the thought of someone seeing a wrinkle coming out of the Tarbell house. "Over my dead body," she always says.

At the far end of the kitchen I veer off left into the laundry room and step around a jumbo Tide and clothes baskets spilling over. Then I squeeze past our old Maytag washer that has a big job ahead of it. My bad leg feels rubbery.

Mother groans. "She's probably dizzy with me having to whirl her every which way to get in here," I tell Barda who bumps me as she slithers past to lift the toilet lid.

"You take care of the laundry then," she growls and lifts Mother's gown as I steady her upright on the floor then lower her onto the seat.

Mother's urine squirts out in tiny spurts, but she smiles, like she has a secret.

"Does that feel better?" Barda says. She pets Mother's hair, pure white and silky fine, which makes Mother twitch.

I mouth to Barda, "You think she can understand?" Mother's had a blank look since her stroke two years ago.

"I doubt it," Barda says.

44

I tip Mother to one side so Barda can wipe her, which she does several times to be sure she won't get a rash. Then she flushes the toilet, my signal to prop her upright while Barda drapes her nightgown around her.

"Don't you think she's hot in that flannel thing? It's May."

"And fifty degrees last night. All she needs is to catch a cold. Besides she's always worn these long nightgowns. She wouldn't feel right without something covering her."

They're the same nightgowns Barda wears except in a size four instead of an eighteen. Once, when I unloaded the washer, I saw Barda's.

I scoop Mother up and Barda lays Mother's head on my shoulder, then walks ahead of me and kneels to push the laundry basket aside and fold a towel. Mother's hair is full of static and tickles my nose. "Pull her hair away from my face before I sneeze."

"For Pete's sake," Barda says, and stands fast, then groans. "Oh no," she says and sinks to her hands and knees. "Not my sacroiliac."

"Just stay there," I tell her and pull my face as far as I can from Mother's angel hair. As I lug her to the living room too fast, I try not to think the worst.

"Barda's down with sacroiliac in the laundry room," I tell Carter. I'm puffing. My legs wobble as I lower Mother onto her bed. She groans.

"Christ Almighty," Carter says. "What the hell we going to do now?"

"I've got my hands full," I tell him, trying to straighten Mother's wadded gown.

Carter pushes and pants his way out of his chair. He had a heart attack last year and has limped since the war. He stumps out, muttering. "God damn it, what next?"

"Who takes care of your mother now that Barda's back is out?" Doris Martin says a few days later in the valley store. I cringe and keep watching Lydia slice my bacon. Bert usually slices it, but he's taken Julia for a check-up.

"Murry? I asked you, who...."

"Carter and me," I tell Doris who walks to the cutting block.

"But I'm sure Barda gave her baths," Doris blabbers on. "Mother Tarbell must be skin and bones. Still, with a bad back, leaning over a tub can be murder."

"Yup," I say. The doctor warned us about keeping Mother clean. Bed sores. And she's starting to stink.

"That's just right," I say to Lydia, nodding toward the meat. Barda wants it not too thick, not too thin. Lydia smells like lilacs.

Doris isn't finished. "Of course, there are three of you to help. Isn't it interesting," she says in that nosy voice of hers. "You three living together all your lives. Never getting away from each other." She laughs. "Must be hard to keep secrets."

"From you," I think to myself but shrug and head off to the tomato bin. Doris shouldn't talk. What kind of secrets can you keep from someone you're married to? Besides, Carter has his weather diary he's kept for forty years. Nobody looks in it. I don't set foot inside Barda's bedroom. No one knows what Mother's thinking. And I have my special locked drawer that even Barda can't see inside when she changes my sheets. Doris doesn't know a thing about secrets.

I wander past the meat and dairy cases, waiting for Doris to leave. I pass the wanted poster tacked to the post office wall of the thieves who came through Timber ten years ago. Later tracked down in Montana for armed robbery. Under it there's a new poster. A blond kid with thin lips and a crooked nose, "Wanted for Murder." He looks nervous, not mean. It's hard to believe he could kill anyone. I won't say that to Carter. He'd say, "You would trust the devil himself."

I glance to the counter, but Doris is still there, yammering on about her niece to Sage, the hippie woman who just came in. Sage finally says she needs to hurry, walks toward where I'm standing and stops at the cooler. "Hi, Murry," she says and smiles in a tired way, like she's just been cornered by a badger. People call Sage's family strange. Her husband Terrill logs with mules and they live in a commune. But as far as I can tell, they don't hurt anybody. And Sage doesn't talk your ear off, something I've liked about her from the first time I met her at Grange.

After Sage leaves, Doris lingers by the valley cookbooks, so I pick up a can of green beans and a couple cans of tuna I plan to put back when she leaves. I have to act busy. As I check out a jar of pickled pig's feet, I hear the door shut. But before I can put things back, Lydia says "You find what you need, Murry?" She's waiting for me.

"Well...yeah sure," I tell her, and hesitate by the shelves. She watches me and smiles. So I walk to the counter where I set the tuna and beans next to my groceries.

"Good sale on that tuna this week," she says. "You're a smart shopper." Yes "smart shopper," is what she says. Her perfume smells different now, without bacon mingling in. Something like gardenias. And she's wearing lipstick.

"That's everything," I say.

She leans toward me. "Don't pay attention to Doris," she says. "You tell Barda I'll stop by and help bathe your mother while her back's mending." She pats my hand.

I pull it back. What would Barda say if she knew Lydia touched me? My face feels hot, and the gardenias smell stronger. "We can get by," I say, then hope I haven't hurt Lydia's feelings by pulling my hand back. But she doesn't seem to mind.

"What are neighbors for?" she says. "I haven't seen Barda since your father's funeral. Twenty-five years ago? And she didn't stay long enough for me to talk to her."

"She was in a hurry," I say, then follow Lydia to my pick-up where she sets a bag of groceries on the seat, then holds the door while I slide mine in beside it.

"Now you tell her I'll come by later in the week."

"You don't need to," I say but she shakes her head.

"It's no trouble." She touches my arm, then waves and disappears into the store.

On the way home I think about how I'll break the news to Barda. What would it be like to have Lydia in the house? It's as easy for her to talk about giving a bath as raising a garden or picking flowers. Just like Miss Harper after my Harley wreck. She had the blondest hair I ever saw—almost white.

The day she gave me a bath she smiled and winked as she walked toward me with a pan I thought was a bedpan. "Now Mr. Tarbell, this isn't what it looks like," she said, set the pan on the floor, then cranked the bed up slowly. I was doped up with pain-killer but could see the pan was filled with soapy water when she lifted it onto the night stand.

"A sponge bath," she said.

I shook my head. Nobody had given me a bath for as long as I could remember. And certainly not a grown woman. "I can do it," I told her.

"With an arm and a leg in casts? You can hardly raise your head." She laughed. "Maybe next time." She circled the curtains around my bed and squeezed out a nubby white face cloth. I'd never seen such a thing. We used rags at home. She started with my face, the area around the bandages that covered the slash over my left eye. "If I'm too rough, tell me," she said.

She rinsed the cloth which had blood from the cut, then carefully lifted off the bandage. "This looks good," she said, and eased that cloth down my good arm. The nubbiness gave me goose bumps.

When she reached my stomach, I tightened up all over. "It's okay," Miss Harper said and started humming "The Old Rugged Cross." We never went to church, but I heard Mother hum it once in a while when she was alone in the kitchen.

When she lifted the sheet completely off me, she hummed louder. I froze up and turned my face away which I could feel was burning up.

She rinsed the cloth, which gave me a chance to grab for the sheet. But it was out of reach.

She kept humming then said, "Now don't worry. I'm used to giving men baths."

I grabbed for the sheet again.

"I'm afraid you'll pull something loose," she said. "Lie quiet. It'll only take a minute. We don't want you getting bedsores. I'm going to take special care to see that that doesn't happen."

"Special care," is what she said. Yes she did.

I didn't move a muscle while she washed my stomach, then slid the cloth down my leg. I tried to keep my mind on "The Old Rugged Cross," that she kept humming: "On a hill far away..." I felt the wash cloth,... "was an old rugged cross..." nubby and warm... "the emblem..." draping itself... " of suffering"... between my privates "and shame"...and Miss Harper's hand.

"Why are you so late?" Barda says when I carry the groceries in the back door. She walks stiff as a board into the kitchen. Her face is pinched as if it hurts to talk.

"Quite a few people at the store," I say. "You don't look like you feel too good yet." I'm thinking this might be the time to tell her about Lydia. But before I can say a word, she's already dug her hand in a sack and pulls out the green beans.

"What's this?" she says. "I didn't have beans on my list." She stares at me. "I put up two hundred quarts last year."

I start toward the cupboard with the cans.

"No," she says. "Right there." She points to the ironing board and pushes some clothes aside. "Set them here, so you can take them back." She glowers. "Couldn't you read my list?"

"Doris Martin grilled me about Mother. She asked how we were bathing her."

"How could she have known?" She stares at me. I shrug.

"Well, I hope you told her we were getting along fine. She'd love to poke her nose in here, pretending to help. That old busybody." She reaches into the bag again. "And tuna?" She holds up the two cans. "Did you gather things up or..." She peers at me over her glasses. "Did that woman take the list?"

"What woman?"

"The one who slipped a couple candy bars in extra for you last time."

"Two-for-one sale. It looked a little overcast on the way home."

"She doesn't have a good reputation you know. She's been married umpteen times and keeps company with younger men."

"She asked about Mother," I say, before she can talk about Lydia's daughter who some say is a prostitute. Why do people like to spread rumors?

"Our mother is none of her affair," Barda says. "I don't see why everybody wants to make our business their business."

"I'll check on Mother," I say and hurry into the living room.

Carter's staring out the window at a cardinal, then looks at me. "You see Lydia?" he says and laughs. Mother frowns.

"Murry's here, Mother," I say. "Murry's here."

I came close to warning them. It was Tuesday and I'd just taken Mother to the bathroom. Carter was holding Mother up on one side. I was on the other. We waited for the spurts. Barda who still can't bend, stood stiff behind us.

"Whew," Carter said. "She stinks like an outhouse." Barda tried to shush him.

"Well, she does," he said.

"Hold her up straighter," Barda said, and pointed at Mother. "She's starting to tip. If she's scared of falling, she can't go."

Carter growled and pushed Mother gently toward me.

"Maybe we should get somebody to help us give her a bath," I said.

"Who? Fran Squaw? You want her nosing around?" Carter said. He's never liked our sister-in-law. He says, "Francoise and her uppity ways. It's all that education. "

"I didn't say Francoise," I told him. "Maybe..."

"Or her preacher friend," he said. "Mr. Praise the Lord. Well, he'll never be praising the lord in this house."

"I'm not having *anybody* nosing around," Barda said.

"P-U," Carter said, wrinkling his nose. "Mother stinks to high heavens."

"I'll be better in a few days," Barda said and shuffled, rigid as Frankenstein, out of the bathroom.

"The doctor warned us about bedsores," I told Carter. "Maybe we should try to find someone to help...besides Francoise. Or Preacher Arlyn."

"Who, your girlfriend?" he said and guffawed.

"I don't have a girlfriend," I told him and let it go. I tried, and it wasn't worth raising the wrath of Barda when there was a chance Lydia wouldn't even show up.

On Thursday, I cringe every time I hear a car on the highway, but when Lydia hasn't come by noon, I start breathing easier. Carter's been watching the news all day, getting steamed up about the thousand tons of bombs the US just dropped on Viet Nam near the DMZ. At about 2:30 he's saying, "We need to get the hell out of there and let them handle their own damned mess," when I see him crane his neck toward the highway. "Who the Hell..."

I hurry to the window and see dust rising off the road. My heart's pounding. Lydia's green 55 Chevy is slowly bumping its way over the gravel. I glance at Barda who's been rocking in her chair, working her crossword puzzle, her feet stuffed into white pumps, rising up then thumping down.

She stops. "Better not be somebody planning to visit," she says. "I'm not dressed for company."

"You look fine, just like autumn," I tell her.

She glares at me, tugs on her green sweater and runs her hands down the skirt of her brown and yellow dress. Then she straightens her white socks that hug her calves so tight, it looks like she doesn't have ankles. Her legs look like alder trunks.

"Who is it?" she says, still staring at me.

"Well...I don't know. Maybe Lydia. She said she might stop by," I say as softly as I can. "To help with Mother."

Carter's standing now, looking out at the dust blowing up from the road.

"Lydia's going to do what?" Barda says, her eyes fiery. "Nobody's coming here to do anything." She tries to get out of her chair. "You tell her we don't need help."

Carter's staring at Lydia who's stepping out of her car. Barda forces herself out of the chair and hobbles over beside Carter. I step up beside her and we watch, as Lydia picks up her purse, changes her mind and throws it back onto the seat. Then she tucks the keys in the pocket of her skirt which is purple and white and black all swirled together. Her blouse is the color of cream when it rises.

"Wearing a blouse with eyelets all over," Barda says. "Disgraceful. You can almost see through it."

"Almost," Carter says.

Lydia looks toward the window and waves.

"Get away from the window," Barda says. "We look like crows on a fence." She shuffles to her chair, which she collapses into with a groan. "She's *your* problem," she hisses to me. She lowers her voice. "You get rid of her. We don't need help. We can..."

Knock. Knock. Lydia looks through the glass panes in the door, smiling and waving.

I'm almost to the door, still trying to think what to say, when she opens it and steps in. "I can let myself in," she says. "Good to see you." She closes the door and stands for a minute looking around. Seeing her stand all bright and colorful makes me see how plain everything is. Faded wallpaper. Brown linoleum squares. Old wood stove.

Then she smiles and looks at Barda. "I haven't been in this house for...well I guess it's been years," she says. "Ever since right after your dad built it."

She walks to Barda who doesn't move a muscle, and she stoops as if she might hug her. Barda pulls back and sticks out her hand which Lydia takes and holds between hers. "You know, Barda, I think you were making a dress that day," she says. "A beautiful dress of little yellow daisies. I thought it was the prettiest dress I'd ever seen. You gave me a cookie. You remember?"

Barda shakes her head. "I...I'm not sure...A dress..." She pulls her hand back, blinks, then glares at me to do something.

I stand by Mother, trying to think what to do, and have just opened my mouth to say Mother's asleep, that we shouldn't bathe her today, when Lydia steps over to Carter who holds out his hand automatically, like he's in a trance.

"And I remember you were out in the shop in your ammunition room," she says. "Is that what you call it?"

He nods. "Well the loading room," he mumbles.

"That's exactly what you were doing, loading shells, and I thought how smart you were to know just how much powder to use so you wouldn't blow yourself up." Then she laughs. "I don't expect you to remember that. It was a long time ago."

Carter clears his throat and sits up straighter. "There's nothing to loading shells," he says.

"It impressed me," she says.

She walks over by Mother. "And your mother was baking blueberry pies. She was so tiny." She reaches down and touches Mother's forehead.

Barda clears her throat then squirms in her chair.

"She's lucky to have all of you to take care of her," Lydia says. "You've done such a wonderful job." She looks at Barda. "She's been sick like this for how long?"

Barda shrugs and slumps.

"Two years," I say. "But we don't want to trouble you. We..."

"It's no trouble at all," she says. She looks again at Barda who's trying to force herself up, out of her chair. She isn't groaning, but her face is tight and pained.

"We can manage," Barda says. "My back's getting back to..."

"Murry said you wouldn't want me to help," Lydia says, touching Barda's arm. "But I told him, 'What are neighbors for?' Your mother sent over pies when my father was sick. It means a lot to have good neighbors."

Lydia strokes Mother's forehead again, then says, "How do you usually get her into the bathroom? Wheel the bed?" She looks underneath.

"We carry her," Carter says, grunting and groaning his way to the edge of the chair, as if he was a part of the 'we.'

"*I* carry her," I say and nod toward Carter. "Bad heart, you know."

"I *could* carry her," Carter says.

Lydia smiles at him. "I'm sure you could," she says, moves to the side of Mother's bed and leans over as if she might lift her.

"I'll get her," I say

Barda shakes her head. "We don't need help." But I'm already pulling Mother to a sitting position and Lydia's wrapping Mother's robe around her. Barda struggles to get up, but Lydia says, "Don't worry. I think I remember where the bathroom is. I had to go and you showed me. Keep working on your crossword." She leans over toward Barda and shakes her head. "I never could get those things." Then she heads out of the living room and quickly through the kitchen.

I balance Mother in my arms and start to follow Lydia, as Barda snarls, "We don't need help." But I hurry toward the sound of water running in the bathroom. I zigzag among the baskets of clothes faster than usual, as I hear Barda's chair creak.

In the bathroom, Lydia smiles and starts to pull Mother's nightgown off as soon as I stand her upright. I stare toward the tub while Mother stands there, without a stitch on. Steam's rising and bubbles tickle my nose. I spot an empty Lily of the Valley packet on the sink.

"What's all that foam?" Barda says. She walks across the room and glares into the tub.

"Bubble bath," Lydia says. Mother's still standing, naked. I keep staring at the sink as I hold her steady.

Lydia turns the water off, sticks her finger in, then jerks it out. "Too hot," she says, turning on the cold.

Mother starts to shiver.

"I hope she doesn't catch cold," Barda says.

"We certainly don't want that," Lydia says and drapes Mother's bathrobe around her, then picks up her dirty nightgown from the floor and hands it to Barda.

Barda holds it a minute, then shuffles out mumbling something about buttinskis. I glance at Lydia who keeps right on with her business. She dips her finger in the bubbles, turns off the cold, and smiles at me. "Ready?" she says, unwrapping Mother. I lift Mother into the tub.

"She's not used to those bubbles," Barda says, clumping back in.

Lydia smiles. "Something new. Right, Mother Tarbell?" Mother starts to moan, then wiggles and sniffs. "Do you have a wash cloth?" Lydia asks Barda.

"Mother's not used to wash cloths," Barda says, her voice hard as river granite.

"Just as well," Lydia says and dunks the corner of a towel into the water. "This works fine."

Mother starts to whimper again.

"New things scare her," Barda says "We've never used bubble bath."

Lydia scoops up a handful of bubbles and slides them across Mother's arm. "We'll get her used to it slowly," she says. Mother wrinkles her nose and sniffs, then sniffs again. Then she slaps her hand against the bubbles.

"She's making a mess," Barda says. "I hope nobody slips and falls." She's hopping mad. I glance at Lydia who slides bubbles down Mother's other arm then gently washes her face and neck.

"That bubbly stuff could get in her eyes," Barda says. When Mother slaps the water again, Barda steps up to the tub. "Mother's not used to strangers."

I give her a nasty scowl, but she scowls back. My heart's racing, and for some reason before I know it, "The old Rugged Cross" is coming out of my mouth in croaky "dah dah dahs."

Barda mumbles, "All this noise will scare her," but Lydia says, "Now that's one I haven't heard in years." She rubs more bubbles over Mother's arm, then over her tiny wrinkled back and shoulders and chest. I turn my eyes away, but keep humming and now Lydia's humming, too. All at once Mother lets out a low howl, like dogs when they hear coyotes. She wants to join in.

"She's scared," Barda snaps, but her voice is drowned out by Mother's splashing and her next howl. Then Barda stomps out of the bathroom.

Lydia keeps dipping the corner of the towel into the warm foamy water and washing, washing while Mother howls to my humming. Finally, Lydia reaches under the bubbles and starts washing the lower parts. I hum louder, but all of a sudden Mother's quiet. When I glance at her, she blinks, then giggles. I look at the sink.

Lydia says, "We're almost done, Mother Tarbell. Almost done." The bubbles have disappeared.

When I carry Mother into the living room, Barda's working on her crossword puzzle and doesn't look up.

"Feel better, Mother? Sure smells better," I say to Lydia.

She touches Mother's hair. "We had a good time, didn't we Mother Tarbell?"

I look at Barda whose lips are so tight I wonder if her mouth could explode.

"Well, I've got to be going," Lydia says and walks over to Carter who reaches out his hand again.

"Nothing to loading those shells," he says. "Nothing to it."

"You'll have to give me a lesson sometime," she says, then wishes Barda well on her puzzle and hesitates. But only for a moment. Barda isn't going to talk. "Well, see you at the store, Murry," Lydia says to me. I open the door for her, then follow her onto the porch where I thank her and stand as long as I can while she walks away.

As soon as I step into the house and close the door, Barda lights into me. "How dare you? Bringing that woman in here, nosing around in our business. Asking if we have wash cloths. As if the way we do things isn't good enough."

I look at Carter who's swiveled toward the window, watching Lydia drive away.

"What you put Mother through. If she catches cold, it'll be your doing."

Carter swivels back toward us. "Nothing to loading those shells," he mutters.

Mother lets out a funny little moan. I cross the room to her bed, but she isn't frowning. And she smells sweet.

"All that foam scaring Mother to death," Barda says, her eyes blazing. When I walk out of the living room, she's going on about what kind of woman puts bubble bath in the water.

I open the door to the upstairs and as I start climbing, notice they're gray near the rails but treaded down to the pine in the center. I'm wondering how many times I've climbed these steps when Barda hollers, "Murry, where are you going? Mother will have to go to the bathroom any minute."

I start humming, "The Old Rugged Cross" and keep climbing.

"You know we can't carry her," Barda yells, but I don't stop. The steps dip in the middle. All those decades of climbing.

In my room, I notice the smell of urine. No doubt from years of using a jar in the night. I look at the windows with no curtains, the chipped gray paint on the walls, the brown floors. Sixty years in an eight by ten bedroom. It's seemed big enough till now. I run my hand over the old brown blanket on the bed. Barda doesn't believe in fancy coverlets. "A waste of money," she calls them.

Then I open my special drawer with my thirty watches including the Seiko Dad gave me for my eighteenth birthday and the pen knife I used for carving logging scenes before arthritis got my fingers and my blue ribbon for taking first in the hundred-yard dash in the eighth grade.

I lift out the wooden box that holds Miss Harper's engagement picture I cut out of the paper thirty-five years ago. I open it and shake her carefully onto the bed. Then I pick her up by the crinkled yellowing edge and tape her to the top drawer of my dresser. Right on the front.

Barda will be yelling, "Hurry, Murry" any minute, but I lie on my bed that creaks every time I move and hum "The Old Rugged Cross." In the night if there's any moonlight, I'll look up, just as I did in the hospital, and there'll be Miss Harper, smiling down at me. Yes, she will.

Hippies

Sage

1973

As Moonbeam and Harvest pack their car for Wisconsin. I try to hide my relief. Our three-year-old Stephen cries and Terrill looks sad while I'm thinking, "Thank God. No more commune. We're finally on our own." But when the car pulls away, I feel a strange dread. I'm four months pregnant and realize how lonely I am.

When we walk into the house, Terrill lifts Stephen up beside him on our wooden bench and strokes his hair. "We'll be all right," he says. "We'll just miss Moonbeam and Harvest for a while." Stephen wriggles his fingers through Terrill's beard.

"Maybe we'll be out there and can visit them," I say. "You know, we don't have to stay here forever." I look at Terrill who smiles, as if I'm making a joke, then sets Stephen down. "Play with your horses and wagon. We'll eat in a little while," he says.

Stephen walks to his toy box and pulls out the logging truck Terrill made him. "Rrrr, rrr," he says but with less enthusiasm than usual. He slides it across the bare boards, the floor our little group danced on when we first moved in. On my twenty-third birthday, we bopped and twisted till three in the morning. I still like the feel of smooth boards under my feet on a chilly morning, but there's been no dancing for a long time.

"Rrr, rrr." A pause, then "rrr, rrr."

Terrill nods in his direction. "He'll be okay. It'll take me a little longer."

I nudge him. "I'm serious. We don't have to stay. Six years is a long time. We're just blowin' in the wind. Remember?"

"I like where we've landed, though." He takes my hand and traces my palm lines.

I marvel that those hands fall twenty-ton firs and coax mules to drag logs through the woods.

"Sage of the long life," he says. "Brave pioneer; adventurer."

"Maybe not so brave," I mumble and pull my hand away. In Madison, when the seven of us hatched the plan to head west where we'd live off the land, Terrill resisted. His cabinet-making business was taking off and he wanted to stay.

"Willow says we can convert the place to a selective logging community," I'd told him. "And Moonbeam read that that area has the lowest church attendance in the country. No born-agains to intrude on our spiritual quest."

"With seven people living up close, it's not a single quest," he said. "And how can we trust Harvest's father not to sell the place out from under us?"

"Harvest says he's mostly hot air," I told him, and didn't admit I was uneasy about her father who'd handed Harvest the deed and warned her, "Three acres of timber won't support one of you, let alone seven. And no matter what fancy ideals you have, folks out there'll consider you a bunch of damn draft dodgers. But your mother wants to let you try. I'll give you a year."

He was wrong about the year but not about our permanence. Garrett, a potter and conscientious objector, survived ten months. A Quaker, he loved the Oregon trees, but not Willow. When she started staring at him as he wedged his clay and laid her head on his shoulder in the evenings, he fled to an Alaskan village where, the last we heard, he was doing odd jobs and helping an old villager mush his dogs. I missed Garrett. He had gentle humor and could fix anything. His leaving left a hairline crack in my dream.

Soon Willow's interest waned. She said her sister needed help with her kids, just temporarily. But in a couple months, she wrote to say her sister needed her indefinitely and to please send her clothes and books.

"Who would have thought we'd be the last to go?" I tell Terrill.

"I'm surprised I made it through the first year with Lennie the Rainbow."

I laugh. "Rainlenbow for a while. Remember how he wanted to knock out walls to enhance the communal sense?'"

"Not even separate bedrooms. He said I was possessive for wanting *us* to have privacy."

"And you said, 'Our intimacy's not for viewing.'" I kiss his cheek. "I loved you for that." I take his hand and run my finger across his lifeline, short and broken. "These things are crazy. Who's the one who never gets sick and wants to stay?"

He looks at me, as if it's sunk in. "You really want to leave?"

"Well, I'm not sure. Not exactly." I think of the people who'll quiz me about our plans when I go to the valley store. "But with the house sold and baby coming, how can we stay?"

His shoulders sag. "Why have I gotten so attached?"

"You always fit in. People take to you. But what's left for us? We've not converted a soul to selective logging."

"I've never believed in converting anybody," he says. "Leaving might be the smart thing. But I'd miss everyone."

I trace his lifeline and think about who I'd miss. Maybe Lydia, but that's more admiring than missing. A woman sleeping with a younger man and raising her granddaughter whose mother's a prostitute in Alaska? Even hippies can't top that.

"These people aren't ever going to change." I glance at Stephen who's helping Babe pull his truck. "We'll always be the damned hippies from up on the mountain," I whisper to Terrill, then push myself up from the bench and walk through what used to be the wall into the kitchen.

We have a month to return the property to a state of normalcy. Harvest's father sold it to a Portland family who will spend weekends in the valley until they log the land. "They'll clear cut it for sure," I told Terrill and wished I could laugh over the irony. But I've not been laughing much lately. Even before Moonbeam and Harvest left, they weren't great company. Eager to move, Harvest grew increasingly bitter with each job rejection. On one occasion she told me, "I'm sorry I let people talk me into this."

When I told Terrill, he smiled and said, "No one held a gun to her head. "

"But why can't she be honest and admit she was one of the instigators?"

"Maybe she has more to lose," he said. "She persuaded her father to back us and expected the venture to give her something it didn't." Terrill could let it go.

Once, when Harvest got a rejection from a medical clinic, her 'dream job,' she declared the whole idea a mistake and said her father was right. Moonbeam agreed and kept stirring the tortilla soup she was making for the two of them. We'd abandoned communal cooking after Harvest and Moonbeam decided they were in love.

"How can you say that?" I said. "That means everything we've done hasn't meant a thing. And you can't determine what's a mistake for somebody else."

"Maybe it's different for you," Harvest said, sprinkling cilantro in the soup as Moonbeam continued to stir it with the wooden spoon Garrett carved before his escape. "You have Terrill and Stephen. Those of us in health care can't take a hiatus without falling behind." Harvest picked up the rejection letter from the counter and flipped it with her finger. "Dropping out of life has cost me plenty."

"You found each other," I said.

"I would have found Moonbeam sooner by staying at Planned Parenthood instead of wasting two years on Lennie the jerk. This detour's led nowhere."

I obsessed on our conversation for days. How could anyone know how a different path would have turned out? How could you regret your life? But if I stay in the valley, I wonder if I'll end up regretting mine. Ever since I found out I was pregnant, I've been thinking about Madison and my sister Olivia.

When I told her about Harvest's comment, she said, "They wouldn't be together if they'd stayed in Madison. Obviously they knew each other there, and Harvest preferred Lennie the jerk. Good riddance to them." Then she said she missed me. I miss her, too.

By Tuesday of the third week after Harvest and Moonbeam leave, we run out of flour and rice and milk. I've stretched them so I wouldn't have to go to the store. I think briefly of sending Terrill, but he's just come in from tearing down the leaky lean-tos Lennie threw together with canvas and wire for Moonbeam's menstrual purification ritual. I've finished most of what I can do—scrubbing walls that are still intact and packing books and papers.

As I make the list for the store, Terrill tackles replacing the stud that Lennie sawed in two. Lennie didn't have a clue how a house held together. He only knew he wanted everyone to be closer. One day, during our first year, after Terrill headed to the woods, Lennie decided to saw the studs out. He said, "They impede my view of people in the kitchen when I'm in the living room." By then, many of the walls had been removed. I said that removing studs would cause structural damage and asked him to wait till Terrill came home.

"Terrill this, Terrill that," he said. "Since when is Terrill the Guru of the house?" I said he wasn't but that I didn't think Harvest's father would like it. But Harvest, who was enamored with Lennie, said, "Who cares what that capitalist thinks?"

I was desperate so fell back on Lennie's hero. "T S. Eliot wouldn't like it," I said. "If we remove vertical studs so everything's horizontal, we're symbolically removing the intersection of the finite and infinite. The mortal and divine." Then I walked nonchalantly through a wall into the kitchen and started cooking. He held off but by then had damaged the stud.

"You need anything from the store?"

Terrill stops pulling at the old stud. "A half-pound of three penny nails. Can we add it to the bill?"

"We're two hundred into them now. Bert said we had to pay before charging anything else." I think about how, when we first moved to the Valley, people's suspicions made me feel like a rebel who stood for something. I imagined that people would eventually respect us, think us courageous. Lately, I feel like an outsider who never got off probation.

"I don't want to ask him for anymore," I tell Terrill. I look in the money jar and count the scattered bills. "Twenty-nine dollars between us and the poor house." I fold the money carefully and put it in my wallet.

"Don't worry," he says. "Skip the nails. I'll get the check from the mill for the load of spruce at the end of the week. That'll last through the month. We'll be okay."

I nod but feel uneasy and wonder if my angst is affecting the baby. Will it be colicky? How could I handle that on top of everything else? I kiss Stephen who's scribbling with a green crayon. "Mama will be back soon," I tell him.

"Ribbet," he says.

Outside it's overcast. I hug my sweater close against the chill and think how a fall day feels in Wisconsin. Warmer maybe. And woods of elm and maple and birch, ready to turn.

Though I love the Oregon woods, I miss Midwest autumns.

I study our VW bus with its flowers and rainbow that Lennie painted. How did we expect to fit in by standing out? I open the door, dented during Willow's 'learning to use a stick shift' phase, and slide into the seat of the van Moonbeam overheard valley gossip Doris Martin refer to as a hippie van. Later when I ran into Doris at the store, she said, "I see you drove the van." I nodded and said, "The hippie van? I've noticed Bert drives one, too. Probably an old hippie."

She looked indignant. "You could hardly call Bert a hippie. He uses it to haul groceries from Mills Port," she said and strode out of the store. Terrill found her reaction amusing, but I found it alienating.

I zigzag my way down the mountain, and on the last hairpin curve, pump the brakes, the way I've done for a couple months. I didn't grow up with vehicles that needed their brakes pumped. How does being short on money free you from anything?

In the store I spot Irene Jenkins, leaning over the freezer. I quietly make my way to the side room stacked with fabrics and sewing supplies. As I pass the counter, Julia looks up from her *Thirty-Three Candles* romance and says, "Hello," in that formal tone that makes me wonder if she's always been distant or only since the accident.

In the back room I rifle through cotton prints and consider buying two yards of chintz covered with turtles. Stephen would like that. I've done a lot of sewing since moving to the valley. I made skirts for Moonbeam and Harvest until recently and all of Terrill's shirts and Stephen's clothes. It was my contribution to the group. I like seeing my clothes on people I love. I finger the fabric, then think of packing. I return it to the shelf and slip out into the main store and to the grains. I pick up ten pounds of flour, five of rice, then try to sneak to the counter. But Irene sees me and scurries over.

"I hear your friends moved," she says in a syrupy voice. "And the house sold. Will the owners move right in?"

"In a few weeks." I turn to Julia who's pulling down our bill. "Cash," I say, wanting Irene to hear. We always pay our bills but occasionally have to ask for an extra week. Paying late is the kind of 'news' I suspect has become valley history.

Irene sets a box of vanilla ice cream bars on the counter. "Someone said Terrill was fixing the place up. Places do get run down after a while, don't they? And with so many people living there."

"Only five of us this last year."

"That Marshall place *was* so cute."

I cringe. That property will always be the Marshall place no matter who lives there.

"I loved the green wallpaper in the bathroom. So fresh and springy."

"It's gone," I tell her and watch Julia reach slowly under the counter for a sack. Why couldn't Lydia be working today? She would have things bagged up by now. I focus on Julia and hope Irene notices I'm in a hurry. But she stands her ground, maybe wanting me to confess that I loved that wallpaper, too; the paper Harvest convinced Moonbeam to paint black to enhance meditation.

"Where will you move to?"

"Not sure yet," I say, holding the sack while Julia struggles to fit the flour in it.

"Not many places for rent around here. And being pregnant and all has got to be a worry. If you stayed, would Terrill still log?" She takes a step closer and catches the bag with the flour that starts to tip while I hold the second bag Julia's clumsily filling.

"It's up in the air," I tell her, folding down the top of the filled sack and pulling it toward me. "We'll have to see."

"Up in the buffalos," Julia says and is just balancing the broccoli atop the bag of rice when Francoise walks in. I fold down the top of the second bag, hoping Irene will pursue Francoise and I can make my escape. But Francoise only nods at her former mother-in-law and slips to the other side of the store. Rumor has it that if it weren't for Darla, Irene would shun Francoise. Irene doesn't share her sons easily. But who really knows? Rumor has it that we hippies all slept together. How could anyone imagine I would sleep with Lennie the Rainbow?

I hug my bags to me and take a step toward the door. But Irene grips my arm and hollers to Francoise who freezes, then turns and walks slowly toward us. At least she looks as unwilling as I feel.

"Hello, Irene," Francoise says, then nods at me.

"Sage's family is looking for a place to live. Do you know of any vacancies?"

Francoise frowns and shakes her head. "Not off hand." Then she turns to me. "We heard the house sold. When will the new owners move in?"

My heart pounds and the groceries grow heavy. Next time, I'll send Terrill. I mumble, "I'm not sure. I'm in a rush today to get back with lunch for Terrill. He's fixing the house." I nod at Francoise, who opens the door for me and smiles kindly. Though I've not gotten to know her, I feel a surge of gratitude.

But Irene isn't finished. "Wait," she says. "Francoise, do you think Arlyn would have something? There are a couple empty houses on his place."

"I'm not sure he's interested in renting," Francoise says. "But...well, I could ask."

"Oh wouldn't that be nice. Arlyn's acreage is lovely," Irene says, as if she's an admirer who hasn't participated in his crucifixion.

I force a smile. "Thanks, but let me check with Terrill before you go to the trouble," I say to Francoise and walk as calmly as I can to the van. But once inside, I go limp and realize I'd hoped for an out. How could I live near Arlyn? I could count on Francoise to hold off, but would Irene be able to keep her nose out of it?

I drive home thinking what Terrill might say. I can't imagine he'd want to live next door to a religious fanatic though he'd probably remind me that Arlyn was the only one in the valley who visited Lannie Mullins in prison after he killed his wife. And surely Arlyn wouldn't be happy about letting us live 'in sin' on his property. If only I'd escaped the store a minute earlier.

I pull the van over at a turnout, roll down the window and inhale deeply. The sky's cleared enough to see the outline of St. Helens above the tree line. She's stood alone for centuries. Is she lonely? I laugh. To think a mountain has feelings. Terrill would say it does. People in the valley would say, "That's a hippie for you."

I lay my head back against the seat. Why couldn't I just tell Terrill I don't fit here? Why couldn't I say, "Irene's nosy and Doris is rude." He couldn't blame me for not getting close to Julia.

It seems easy for him. The first time we met the Mullins boys, John Mullins boomed out, "Hear you're using a team of mules. Couldn't you find a slower way of logging?" Then he poked his older brother, Nathan, who guffawed.

Terrill laughed, too. "That's about as slow as it gets," he said. Then he walked over to John and said he'd probably be coming around with questions as he was new at this whole thing. The Mullins kept laughing, but Terrill had slid away from the jab, hadn't let it get to him. When his logging started paying off, people quit laughing. When his equipment broke, he could depend on the Mullins for help.

It's Terrill's going his own way and letting others go theirs that drew me to him. He's an inch shorter than I am, which doesn't bother him in the least. He likes simple joys. What are my joys? Taking Stephen on walks where I point out alder and fir bark and gather mushrooms and cones. Weaving straw hats for our mules Emil and Susie, and hearing Stephen giggle when we set the hats on their heads. And, of course, listening to coyotes in the night, while I'm curled up next to Terrill.

In Terrill's and my ten years together, I've never kept secrets. Or have I? I haven't confided how unhappy I've felt lately. Maybe I've not realized it till now.

I start the van and vow I'll tell him about Arlyn's houses. I'll admit I don't want to move there, maybe not stay in the valley, period. He'll understand.

"What's new off the mountain?" Terrill says when I walk in. Spaghetti sauce simmers on the stove, and he's almost finished replacing the old stud. "Tomorrow the sheet rock. Then the painting," he says.

"Mama's home," Stephen says from the corner where he's coloring.

I blow him a kiss, walk to the stove and open the lid. "Smells good." I pick up the ladle and stir. "Irene grilled me about our plans and asked Francoise to look for rentals in the valley without even knowing if we'd be staying."

Terrill smiles and stretches to reach the nail he's hammering. "She's funny."

"Nosy is more like it. Acting innocent, like she's trying to help."

"Yeah. Though she did work hard on the benefit dinner when John Mullins died."

I stir the sauce vigorously, as Terrill climbs down from the chair and stands back. "That's better. Doesn't look like it's ready to topple."

"Here," I say and hand him a plate of lettuce and tomatoes through the open wall.

He sets it in the middle of the round table he and Garrett made our first year. "I'm starved," he says then disappears into the bathroom.

"Time to wash for dinner, honey," I tell Stephen who holds up his scribbles. "Emil and Susie," he says.

"Good, honey," I say. "Go show Daddy."

He runs toward the bathroom. I fill the stoneware glasses Garrett gave me with water from the well. Fed by a spring. I'll miss that.

"He sure likes drawing," Terrill says, returning from the bathroom.

"Maybe he'll be an artist," I say. "A good elementary school could take him far."

Terrill nods. "Francoise said Oregon schools are among the best." He lays Stephen's drawing on the fridge. "Shall we show Emil and Susie after dinner?"

Stephen runs to the door.

"Whoa, Paul Bunyan," Terrill says. "After dinner."

"Francoise have any news?" Terrill says when I hand him a plate of spaghetti.

"She didn't seem excited to listen to Irene's grilling."

"Grilling?"

"Hands clean?" I say, inspecting Stephen's fingers when he rests his chin on the table. I lift him into his special chair. "A little wet but clean."

I pass the tomatoes to Terrill. "Just a minute, honey," I tell Stephen when he reaches for them. "There's plenty for everybody."

"Only ten days left," Terrill says. "Things are shaping up though."

"Too bad we couldn't have lived in it fixed up," I tell him. "Remember how Olivia always said that."

"Oh, speaking of Olivia, I forgot she called. She wondered about our plans."

"What did you tell her?" I hand Stephen a paper towel.

"I said we hadn't had time to look but hoped something would turn up."

I feel a knot in my stomach as I take a bite of spaghetti. "This sauce is really good," I tell Terrill. "But maybe could use a bit more oregano."

When Stephen's in bed, I call Olivia "Any jobs your way?" I ask her.

"You can always find something," she says. "People are crying for handy men if Terrill wants to do that. And you can stay with us for as long as you need to. I think it'd be good at least till after the baby comes. There's a new tract opening up five miles from here. One of the best school districts in the state." When I'm quiet, she says, "How you holding up, hon? The truth."

I look toward the bedroom where I assume Terrill's reading and lower my voice. "It's not easy right now, figuring out work and where to live."

"Well, maybe it won't be an issue. The way you've described that place, there's no housing boom." She laughs. "No house, no stay. I'll have Mike start cleaning out the bedroom over the garage. Looks like..."

I glance again toward the door and whisper to her about my encounter with Irene. "I haven't told Terrill yet and I'm feeling guilty."

"You have to watch out for yourself. In that god forsaken place, who'll deliver the baby? And in the winter? Terrill just wants you to be happy." Then she talks about driving Lee and Amy to dance classes and Sara's wanting to play the flute and how she can't devote as much time to PTA with Mike's practice taking off.

"Sounds like you never stop," I tell her and think about their frenzied life that pulls them in every direction. That isn't me. But then I picture her standing in a kitchen with a dishwasher. In a neighborhood with people to talk to during morning walks. Driving her Firebird with brakes you don't need to pump. Near a library where she checks out five books at a time. "You seem happy," I say and feel the baby move. "Did you get bigger with the second one? I'm big as a house."

"Smaller with the second but huge with Sara. She was nine pounds five ounces. Caesarean, remember?"

"Something to look forward to. Harvest delivered Stephen and I felt comfortable having her here. But with her gone, I need to find a doctor. And we'll have to drive over this mountain to the hospital." I think about Julia's accident.

After I hang up, I check on Stephen who's conked out. When I hear an owl hoot, I stare out the window into the dark and wonder if he's the spotted kind that loggers fear will mess up logging when it ends up on the Endangered Species list. Terrill would lobby for the owl, another way we don't fit.

The hoots stop. Maybe he's spotted a mouse, scurrying home to her family. I shiver and hope she makes it. Nothing seems safe. I push myself up from the chair and wander into our bedroom. The room's chilly so I pull a blanket around me and sit on the bed beside Terrill who's reading Emerson.

"You know this guy improves with age," he says. "Listen to this: 'What lies behind us and what lies before us are small matters compared to what lies within us.'"

I twist my braid around to check for split ends. "You know Olivia reminded me she had a Caesarean with Sara. I'm bigger than I was with Stephen."

Terrill glances up then closes the book. He bends over and rests his ear on my stomach.

"What if I have to have a Caesarean? And I don't even have a doctor."

"We still have a few months," he says. "Dunlops' granddaughter just had a baby. I'll find out who their doctor was."

"Shouldn't we wait?"

He frowns.

"I mean in case we leave. I'll get a doctor wherever we end up."

"I'll ask this week about rentals."

"Even if we find a place, with the timber sold, there's no job."

"We'll think of something. He puts his arm around me.

Though I think of telling him about Arlyn's, I decide Olivia's right. I need to think of myself and the baby. But I can't fall asleep for a long time, worrying about it.

On Monday, Stephen and I go to the woods for kindling. Terrill's painting and wants me away from the fumes. When I return, Arlyn's pulling out of the driveway and waves. "I hear we might be neighbors," he says, flashing the smile that, I decided when I first met him, must have won his ex-wife's heart. He has movie star quality. "Terrill will tell you," he says, nodding at Stephen who holds up his three sticks.

My heart pounds. "Oh?" I say, unable to smile.

"You'll start a great fire with those," he says to Stephen, then "God bless you."

Terrill's sitting at the table, a page of figures in front of him when we walk in. "What did Arlyn want?" I ask him, dumping my load by the fireplace.

"He may have a place for us. That is..." he hesitates. "If we want it. He said I could help him log a little, at least till I find something. He has timber and equipment but isn't against my using Emil and Susie." His voice sounds wary, a tone I'm not used to. I glance at him and cringe when I see the hurt.

"He said Irene mentioned his place to you. But you didn't tell me."

I start sweeping the pieces of twigs that litter the floor. "I didn't think you'd be interested, living next to a preacher." I laugh. "What did you tell him?"

"I said I would have to discuss it with you, of course, and look at the place."

"Anybody hungry?" I say and step toward the kitchen.

Terrill reaches for my arm, but I sidestep him. He sits heavily onto the bench, and I can feel him watching me as I fill the kettle.

"Are you afraid I'm going to let you go through having the baby alone?" he says.

I shrug.

"I'll be with you through the whole thing, just like with Stephen. I asked Arlyn about doctors. He's going to check with someone in the Mills Port Clinic."

"Leftover spaghetti?" I say, pulling a pan from the rack.

"We've always talked about things. If it's the baby..."

"It's not just that," I say, setting the pan on the counter and forcing myself to look at him. Then I walk to the rocker and drop into it. "It's...it's the loneliness."

"Arlyn's closer to town than we are here."

"That's just it," I say. "You don't understand."

He leans toward me and shakes his head. "I guess I don't. But I want to."

"These people...these people don't...they're not... I don't have a person I can confide in." I avoid his eyes. "Who am I supposed to talk to? Buffalo woman? Irene or Doris who consider us immoral?"

"They don't mean any harm. They're..."

"You don't know what it's like for me. You spend your days in the woods and don't have a clue how it feels to be looked at askance every time you go to the store or mention you're a vegetarian or talk about fixing the house."

"Fixing the house?"

"You're oblivious," I say. Stephen holds his arms up and I lift him to my lap.

Terrill opens his mouth to speak, then closes it again. He's lost. Finally he says, "You've been miserable all these years and I haven't known?"

I shake my head. "Ever since Harvest and Moonbeam paired up, there's been no one to talk to during the day. And who in the valley do I have a thing in common with?"

"Arlyn likes to garden," he says. "And Lydia..."

"Arlyn...Lydia. They're out...outside what's going on."

"I thought that's why you wanted to move here in the first place. To be away from people who defined how we were. Arlyn's a good sort. Remember how he brought us a load of wood that first winter. And Lydia doesn't let anybody change her. I thought you admired that."

"I do. I'm just not..." I set Stephen down, push myself up and stand squarely in front of him. I feel the anger rising. "Maybe I'm not brave enough to do it. Did you ever think of that?"

"That's not true. You..."

"My idealism has been squashed. I want a community. If we move to Arlyn's, we'll be worse outcasts than we've been on the mountain. He's a pariah. For someone to dump his family to be the fisher of men and have that fish be one or two people... well, you can soften it if you want to, but it's strange."

He's quiet a moment, then says gently, "We don't know all the circumstances."

Stephen who's been clinging to my leg, runs to his little truck and starts revving it up. "You, who were scared of organized religion, now you want to live near a preacher?" I think of the baby. "It's not fair of you to ask..."

He holds his hand up for me to stop, his jaw tightening. "I'm not afraid of Arlyn," he says. "And I didn't want to move here but agreed to because of you. It's not unfair that I've grown to like it." His voice is stern, like when he told Lennie our private life wasn't for viewing. In our years together, he's never been this angry at me.

"I didn't mean..." I say, but stop when I can't think what I did mean.

"Vroom vroom," Stephen says, as Terrill walks out of the room.

The next day we're quiet. As Terrill hangs sheet rock, I rummage through the attic and find a roll of yellow wallpaper I remember seeing when we moved in. It's old and has a crispy feel, but it's good enough to cover the morbidly black bathroom.

I mix the flour and sugar, water and alum and cloves, Harvest's recipe for paste. I have to admit, I've learned a lot about makeshift techniques or 'the original way,' according to Harvest.

"Do you have the tape measure?" I ask Terrill, who hands it to me without making eye contact.

"It looks good," I say, hating the tension. It's how Lennie treated Moonbeam after Harvest fell in love with her. Lennie left shortly after that.

At two, the phone rings. Terrill answers it. "One minute," I hear him say, then footsteps to the bathroom. "It's Arlyn, He wonders what we decided. I assume it's 'no.'"

"I can't make that decision for both of us."

"One is for both." He turns away before I can respond. I suppose he'll tell Arlyn I'm the one who doesn't want to stay. Then everyone can say *I'm* the one who couldn't adjust. Anger rises in my throat. It's not my fault I feel lonely. I tiptoe closer to the living room.

"We've decided we won't be able to take you up on your offer," Terrill says. "With the baby coming and all, we'll probably move closer to family. But we really appreciate it." Then he's quiet, listening. What's Arlyn saying?

"That's very generous," Terrill says. "I'll tell her."

I slip back to the bathroom and wait for him to tell me whatever it is. But he doesn't come in.

At dinner, we talk about the house improvements and I wait for him to mention Arlyn. Finally I can't stand it. "How did Arlyn take the news?" I say.

"He wished us well."

What's he hiding? Maybe Arlyn said something that exposed his strangeness. Terrill's protecting him. He won't give me the satisfaction of admitting the flaws in these people. It's comforting in a way that Terrill has petty moments.

I push the salad across the table to him. "I overheard. You told him you would tell me something."

"That he wished us well," he says without looking at me.

"You're a bad liar."

His face flushes. "He offered us the first two months free, just to get settled. He said he knew how it was, relocating."

I take a bite of salad. "Why wouldn't you want to tell me that?"

He hesitates. "I didn't want you thinking I was trying to coerce you." He puts down his fork and sighs. "I'm sorry about our argument," he says. "I didn't understand how lonely you've been." He reaches for my hand. "It'll take me a little while to adjust to moving back to the Midwest, but it'll be fine."

I feel a mix of relief and uneasiness as he lifts Stephen from his chair and starts clearing the table. He's a better man than I've ever known. And he's right. I'm the one who's not being fair. How can I treat him like this? "I'll do the dishes," I tell him. "You two go feed Emil and Susie."

Something wakes me in the night, maybe an owl or coyote. The room's cold and I think of central heating in Madison. I glance at Terrill, sleeping soundly as usual. Does nothing keep him awake? I shiver and slip from bed then make my way to the cupboard for a quilt Moonbeam made. I can see its bright squares of autumn colors in the light from the 'hole to the universe' Lennie cut in the ceiling that Terrill replaced with a skylight. How could I ever have thought Lennie would be an asset?

Terrill stirs. "What's wrong?"

"Nothing. I'm just getting another blanket."

"Are you cold? Crawl under," he says and pulls back the covers, as I slide the quilt from the cupboard. "Listen," he says.

Yaps of coyotes pierce the night, then stop abruptly. "How do they stop on cue? It's a mystery."

"It's a devious plot to make humans say, 'It's a mystery,'" I say as I slide under the covers.

He laughs. "Such an eerie sound." He reaches for me, but I hug the quilt between us.

"An eerie sound you'll not hear in Madison," I say, feeling my jaw tighten.

He's quiet for a moment. "There are mysteries everywhere," he says. "I read that deer and raccoons are entering cities now. Maybe we'll end up with critters in our yard. Stephen would like that." He starts to remove the quilt, but I hold on.

He places his hand over mine. "*We're* more important than all the animals in these woods," he says. "Did you see Stephen's latest picture of Emil and Susie?"

"Huh uh."

"He drew it on a scrap of that wallpaper. Susie's a purple squiggle and Emil's red. He said the orange circle was Paul Bunyan. That kid. You can never tell what he'll come up with."

"Crisp yellow wall paper for a sketch pad," I say, remembering what struck me when we first moved here. The nights, huddled in bed together, planning how we'd make what we needed or improvise what we couldn't. Terrill embraces the quilt and as much of me as he can stretch his arms around. This man who I've hurt but who forgives me and loves me anyway. Really good people must suffer more because of the rest of us who haven't caught up.

Maybe I've not given the place a chance. In the safety of our bed with the chill air and coyotes outside, we rely on each other. Could I give it a try, the way Terrill did for me? Maybe it'll be different with just us, not Harvest or Rainlenbow or Moonbeam. "I can't say yes for sure," I whisper. "But I guess we can at least look at Arlyn's." Then I pull the quilt from between us, slowly, letting myself sink into his warmth.

Genesis

Lanny

1975

As I watch Janice sleep, I wonder if she ever wakes in the night and is startled to be lying next to a guy who shot his first wife in the breast. A pregnant wife at that. Those years in the pen, I dreamt of bloody milk spilling out of Paula's breast. Not exactly the milk of human kindness. My old man used to say, "Listen, Lanny, there ain't no such thing. Eve soured that milk in Eden. You trust people and you'll end up looking like a damned fool."

I touch Janice's thin brown hair that fans out on the pillow. Her face is fuller now, but she was plump even before she got pregnant.

After my old man met her, he told me, "She sure ain't no Paula." Whether Paula was cheering, "Slug it Big Lan," at my baseball games or shoving her hand in my back pocket when we walked down Main Street, she was a looker. She swung her hips and flipped her hair back from her eyes and winked and smiled at people so they turned red.

Janice moans and her eyelids flicker. She smiles when she sees me looking at her. "How's my handsome man this morning?" she says and kisses my cheek. We've only been married a year. How long will it take her to stop seeing me that way?

She throws her arm over my chest. "Leo's dropping by today. Did I tell you?"

"Nope." We've been back in the valley a month, living behind the feed store. The only person who has stopped by besides Uncle Joe and his lady friend, Lydia, is Arlyn who bought a bag of feed and invited us to church. I remember my old man saying that in high school, Arlyn was a basketball star and strong as a horse. He helped us finish haying, the summer my granddad busted his collar bone when a vine maple knocked him flat.

Arlyn's dad was real holy and loaned him to us for free. Arlyn didn't resent working for nothing. "One of the best kids around," my old man said. "A damn shame he got religion." These days, being around Arlyn isn't a way to make points in the valley. I hinted that to Janice after we moved back and she started going to his church.

Janice kisses me. "I ran into Leo at the Store. He told me he was out of feed."

"Was Doris with him?"

"No."

"I didn't think so."

"She'll come around. It takes time," she says and snuggles close. "Love you."

"Love you, too." I pull her against me. How can she have such faith in people after working as a prison nurse, my nurse when I had shingles? She believed in me right away and swallowed my lawyer's defense, hook, line and sinker when he said, "It's true, Lanny was stronger than Paula, but that doesn't matter when a gun goes off. He didn't wish her and the baby dead. He was more excited about the baby than she was. He isn't violent but had a horrific accident. It wasn't his nature but his misfortune to kill." I wasn't good at remembering school stuff, but that speech I'll never forget.

When I got out of the joint, Janice didn't blink an eye about marrying me. But her mother was against it. When my old man died and left me the feed store, her mother told her,

"Just because you don't crucify people, doesn't mean others won't. Besides, it's bad luck, moving back to the scene of the crime." Maybe she's right.

Janice rolls to the edge of the bed. "Push," she says and laughs.

I brace my hands against her back while she sits up.

"Don't move your hands or I'll fall and squash you," she says, then twists around to look at me. "How did you sleep?"

"Tossed and turned some."

"I can't believe I only went to the bathroom once. It'll be so nice to sleep through the night again." She gets up very slowly, sways, finds her balance and walks toward the bedroom door. On her way, she stops by the mirror and stands sideways. Then she turns to see herself straight on. "Hey you in there," she says. "You know how you're making me look?" She turns and grins at me. "I can hardly bend over."

"Can I do something?"

"You want to carry me everywhere?" She laughs and waves as she walks out.

Paula laughed a lot when we started dating our freshman year and kept laughing all through high school. She called me Biceps and Slugger. She said, "You're awful," but giggled when I told her the latest trick I'd pulled on Barry McGee, a scrawny kid I called Fairy McPee.

If she wasn't laughing, she was fussing over me. Like the time she got all worried when I told her my old man was pushing me to enlist, saying Viet Nam would make a man out of me. She said, "Marry me and I'll make a man of you."

But just a couple months after we got hitched, she was acting mad all the time. "Why don't you buy brand jeans instead of *those* ugly things?" "Why did you let the barber cut your hair so short? You might as well join the Marines." "Do we always have to watch *Gunsmoke*? We never go out." Right before she found out she was pregnant, she said, "Everyone's at college having a great time, and I'm stuck in this hick place."

I didn't know what to say. I started buying Levis and told the barber, "Not too short." I went wherever she wanted to Saturday nights, even though I knew the guys from high school would say, "Pussy whipped worse than Romeo."

I even ignored my old man who warned me, "Don't give in. A woman doesn't like a wimp." But what could I do? Being around Paula made me feel good. I loved touching her and having sex and being naked beside her in the night. I wanted her to laugh at my jokes again and say that seeing me in a tee shirt turned her on.

But no matter what I did, she wasn't happy. And once she was pregnant, it got worse. One night I heard her crying. "My stomach," she said. "It'll never be the same."

"You look good to me," I said and tried to give her a hug.

"Don't," she said. "You can't even get your arms around me."

"Yes I can," I said and told her I loved her. I was hoping she would say she loved me, too. It'd been a long time. I tried to put my arms around her again.

"Don't," she said, louder this time. "Everything's so boring."

Before Janice leaves for work, I have her close her eyes then lead her to the shop at the back of the store. I've been fixing it up in my spare time. "A place to strip furniture, and bring in extra cash," I tell her when she opens her eyes. "It'll be away from the house so the fumes won't get to you and the baby."

"You sure about this? You hated doing that before." She doesn't say, "In prison."

"That's because I was working for somebody else."

"Just so you don't think you have to. We're doing okay."

"Not on what I'm making." I think of Irene Jenkins and Doris Martin, shaking their heads over my getting out of the pen. They probably wish Oregon still had the death penalty. "I've only had three customers total since we got here."

"You sell things Bert doesn't carry at the store. Business will pick up."

"Maybe. But I want you and the baby to have what you need."

"We'll be..."

"I need to stay busy."

She hugs me. "Just don't turn into a workaholic. Otherwise, who's going to give me foot massages and back rubs? And change the diapers?"

"Diapers?" I say and grin. "Stripping furniture sounds better all the time."

An hour after she leaves, Leo comes by. He climbs out of his pickup, slower than I remember, and he's lost most of his hair. He nods at me as he closes the pickup door. He looks kind of nervous.

"Ran out of Omeline," he says when he walks toward me. "For the calves. Thought you might have some."

"Picked up two bags day before yesterday," I tell him and head back toward the store. His steps are slow on the gravel. I wonder if Doris knows he's here. Paula cleaned her house a few times while she was getting over gall bladder surgery, and she testified against me at the trial. She said, "Paula was vulnerable and sweet and needed attention." When the lawyer asked if she knew of any trouble between us, Doris said "Paula didn't seem happy and told me once, 'Lanny wishes I'd never gotten pregnant.'"

Doris doesn't know that I said that after Paula told me being pregnant ruined her life and it was my fault. But what Doris said really didn't matter anyway. The lawyers twisted everything. By the time it was over, there were two stories: In one, Paula was a nice, pregnant girl, standing by her fireplace one minute and murdered by her horrible husband the next; in the other, Paula was a lunatic, waving her gun around at "an understandably distraught husband," who accidentally shot her when he grabbed for it.

I lift the fifty-pound bag of grain off the shelf.

"I'd forgotten how fast my calves go through this stuff," Leo says as I drop the bag on the counter. "How much I owe you?"

"Twenty."

He pulls out a bill.

"The price has gone up," I say, knowing he can get it cheaper at the Mills Port Feed. They buy in bulk.

"Saw Janice at the Store," Leo says as he hands me the twenty. "She still working over the mountain at the hospital?"

"Yup." I say and figure as soon as Doris finds out, she'll be badmouthing me for making Janice drive over the mountain in her condition.

"Do you remember that dump up there on the mountain?" Leo says.

"Dump?"

"You were probably too young. Everybody just drove up the mountain—about three miles—and threw their garbage into the canyon. Now the state would have your head for that. Everything's gotten legalized. Doris and I have recycled for years but not their way." Leo leans closer as if someone might be listening. "We've always fed scraps to the cats or the cows and buried food that they wouldn't eat under the fruit trees. We've dropped everything else in the burn barrel. Now they say, 'Plastic fumes hurt the air. You can't burn this time of year. You can't do this and that.' So now they want to pick up all that stuff and haul it to the cities where they do something with it."

"They have a recycling plant in Salem," I tell him then wish I hadn't. I was on the recycling crew my first year in the pen. "Your plan probably works better."

Leo shifts his weight. "All I know is, once the law sticks its nose in, it costs twice as much and is half as good." He starts to pick up the bag. "You ever notice that?"

I feel my face burn. "I'll get it."

"I can," Leo says but lets go of the burlap. He never let anybody help him before his bout with prostate cancer. My old man said that took something out of him.

I throw the bag over my shoulder. "You still logging?"

"Retired. After forty years. Time slips by and you're old. The strangest thing." He glances at me. "Sorry about your dad. Darned heart attacks."

"Yup." Maybe Leo thinks I killed him, the way Doris thinks I killed my mother. After Mom's funeral, Doris sent a card to my old man saying something about my mother dying of a broken heart. He never came to visit me but read it over the phone.

When we get to the pick-up, Leo points to the back. I toss the bag in. "You're still strong as a horse," he says.

I shrug. Maybe he thinks prison makes you soft.

That night Janice comes home dead tired and flops onto the couch.

"Just closed a few minutes ago," I tell her. "I wish you could take it easy. Once I start refinishing..."

"I'm okay, hon," she says and yawns. "Did Leo come by?"

"Um hm."

"What did he know?"

"Not much. I wonder why he really came?"

"Probably needed feed," she says and groans when she bends to unlace her nursing shoes.

"I'll get those." I untie the laces then start rubbing her feet.

"Oh that feels good. You're so good to me," she says and leans her head against the back of the couch. "I almost feel too tired to go to Arlyn's tonight."

"Don't go. I'll make dinner, we'll watch tv..."

"Arlyn's doing something special for the baby," she says and looks at me.

"I'll start dinner," I say and head to the kitchen. "Do you want..."

"Lanny?"

"Chicken or I could bake salmon..."

"Would you? Oh I know it's a lot to ask...never mind."

I wait a minute then tell her how Leo said they used to dump garbage up on the mountain. I start the water boiling.

I hear her groan and shuffle toward the kitchen. I pull out the frying pan and when I set it on the stove, feel her arms around my waist.

"Do you think you could drive me to Arlyn's? I'm bushed for some reason."

"Well..." I turn and look at her. I can just hear Doris say, "Poor Janice has to drive over that mountain in her condition and Lanny won't even take her to church."

"Sure. I guess. Yeah okay," I tell her, but a bad feeling's crawling right up my gut.

When I pull onto Arlyn's mile long lane, I remember he really is off the beaten path. My old man used to say that that described more than where Arlyn lived. Francoise's car is already there and suddenly my heart pounds like a bad piston. I can't go in. I'll drop Janice off and come back for her in an hour.

But when I stop, Janice leans over and kisses me. "This means so much," she says. "It's a special night for us with the baby." She steps out of the car and waits, then leans down and looks into the open window. "You okay?"

"Sure." I slide out. "Just so I don't have to say anything."

She slips her arm through mine as we walk up the blocks of cement Arlyn uses for a sidewalk. The yard has a few clumps of grass but mostly dead weeds and dirt.

Arlyn opens the door before Janice can knock. "Welcome to the house of the Lord," he says. "It's nice to see *both* of you." He points toward the living room. "Make yourselves at home. I have to gather up a few things. Be back in a minute." Before he heads into the other room, I notice two buttons are missing from his shirt. Maybe he doesn't have a needle or thread. Or maybe, living alone, he doesn't care how he looks.

I step into the huge room. I've only been here once, years ago as a kid after his family left him. The place was a log house, and I gawked at the hundred-foot fir stretched the length of the room as a ceiling beam. My old man poked me and said, "Hey, kid, your mouth a fly trap?"

I follow Janice across the wood floors to the frayed rug in front of the fireplace. Francoise sits in the row of straight back chairs Arlyn uses for furniture. He isn't one for fancy things. And maybe when Bethany left, Arlyn never replaced what she took.

When she sees me, Francoise smiles and says hi, then hugs Janice. "You're looking more like a mom every time I see you," she says. She doesn't say I look like a dad. Maybe she's thinking I would already be a dad if I hadn't killed Paula. "How are you feeling?" she says and touches Janice's stomach.

"Tired tonight. I conned Lanny into bringing me."

I cringe and Francoise blinks.

"How much time will you take off when the baby comes?"

"A month, then Lanny'll babysit in the store until business picks up."

"Oh," Francoise says, then looks at me.

"You still teaching?" I ask her.

She nods.

"She was my teacher," I tell Janice. "What's Darla doing these days?"

"Teaching at the University of Indiana. Runs in the family, I guess. But I wish she weren't so far away."

"She was real smart," I say to Janice. "She got a scholarship to Japan when she graduated." My voice is shaky. I've never liked groups where you have to keep gabbing so things won't turn quiet.

"I've always wanted to travel," Janice says. "For a while I wanted to join the Peace Corps or go to Haiti as a nurse. But now..." She laughs and pats her stomach.

"There's nothing wrong with helping at home," Francoise says. "The cities are full of people who don't have homes or jobs, and with kids getting into trouble..." She stops and her face turns red. I look at the floor. "Well, there's plenty to do."

I glance at Janice whose face is red, too. But she laughs. "I guess that's why we come to church. To pray for things to get better."

I'm not religious, but I say a quiet "Thank you God," when there's a noise at the door and a scrawny, short man walks in. He nods at everybody then sits in the chair between Francoise and me. A bible's tucked under his arm, and he has hair down to his shoulders and a short beard.

It must be Terrill, the hippie my old man told me about. The fool trying to log with mules.

"Looks like I got here just in time," he says, turns to me and sticks out his hand. It's the smallest man's hand I've ever shaken. His grip's soft even though his hand's firm. In school, we would have used him for bait.

"I'm Terrill," he says and looks me square in the eye.

"Lanny Mullins," I mumble then watch for him to draw back. I'm sure Arlyn must have told him about the shooting.

"Nice to meet you," he says, acting like everything's normal.

"Terrill lives next door," Janice says. "Here at Arlyn's."

"Oh." I remember my old man saying not long before he died, "It's a perfect set-up. Keep all the crazies in one spot." Now here we all are, at church. I look at Janice who's telling Terrill the baby's kicking a lot. She doesn't seem to care that a piece of his hair is braided and tied with a leather string or that his tee shirt says, "Walk her softly: Our Mother the Earth."

"Terra, our second, kicked so much Sage was convinced her rib cage was bruised. It must wear you out," Terrill says then looks at me. "I hear you just moved back."

"Yup," I say, checking his face for a sneer.

Francoise is rummaging through her purse, making a lot of noise.

"I grew up in Madison," Terrill says. "If I moved back, nobody would recognize me. Must be different, returning to a place where everyone remembers you."

"Uh huh," I say just as Arlyn walks in.

"It's so nice to see you," Arlyn says to me. "How is everything going?"

My face feels hot. Why doesn't he leave me alone? Everyone's staring. I mumble, "Fine." I don't like Janice seeing me on the hot seat? Paula wouldn't have come near Arlyn's.

"God bless you," Arlyn says. "I know how it is, being separated from loved ones. It's good to have you back."

I stare at the floor. Arlyn doesn't know a thing about what I've been through. He spent three months in jail for getting behind on child support and saying, "God will provide." It's not the same as killing someone.

"No place is without God's love," Arlyn says. "God is with us no matter what we worry about or fear. As we prepare for Janice and Lanny's baby to join us in this world, it's a good time to offer our burdens up to God. The baby won't be so crowded in there with the worry gone." He smiles at Janice. "Tonight we'll share a burden we'd like to rid ourselves of. Then we'll ask God to help us find strength to do that. Remember Matthew 11:28: 'Come unto me all ye who labor and are heavy laden and I will give you rest.'"

My heart's pounding so hard, I wonder if people can hear it. Francoise squirms in her chair. Maybe she doesn't like unburdening any more than I do. Or maybe she doesn't like sitting in the room with an ex-con.

One summer at church camp I saw this public confession stuff. My old man didn't want me to go to that sissy camp, but for once my mom put her foot down. "It won't hurt him to spend a little time praising God," she said.

In that last testimony service at camp some of the girls were crying and hugging on each other. The minister kept saying, "Is there anyone else who will confess his sins?" I kept telling myself I didn't need to say anything out loud because God knew what I was thinking. But I had an awful feeling that being willing to make a fool of myself in front of everyone would prove I was following God instead of man, which was the camp theme.

As a couple of guys, then quite a few girls stood up and said what they were sorry for and how they were going to turn their lives around, I started thinking about what I'd done to Barry McGee. Things like, "I won't put cereal in Barry's locker again," and even, "I promise not to call him Fairy McPee," kept running through my mind. The thoughts got so strong I held onto my seat for fear I might stand up. Finally, I looked at the back of Paula's head at a curl that was rolling toward the left. She was sitting with her girlfriend, whispering, and I stared at that curl and where it curved and where it touched the next piece of hair. Then I looked at one hair at a time and tried to count them. Some hairs were a little different color than the others, and I stared deeper and deeper into those hairs until everything went blurry. I was looking so hard, I didn't hear the minister say it was time for the closing prayer until Paula's curls bowed.

That next fall, guys at school who went to camp called anyone who confessed Jesus Freaks or Mama's Boys or Goodies. It was a narrow escape, and I never went back. As I look at Arlyn, smiling and ready to go, I start to sweat.

"Let us pray. Dear God, as Janice and Lanny await the arrival of their baby, we want to clear out our worries and fears. We know how hard that is. Let us each look into our heart and find what's burdening us. Touch each of us tonight, Lord, and help us open ourselves to you and to each other. Amen."

"Does anyone want to start?" Arlyn says.

Nobody says anything. All I can think is that Arlyn's talking about *our* baby and Janice will expect me to say something. But how can I admit I'm worried about everything? The store, being back in the valley, Janice changing her mind about me. I'm thinking maybe if nobody says anything, Arlyn will preach. I actually pray for a sermon.

"I'll start then," Arlyn says which makes me breathe easy for a minute while he tells us how hard it was when Bethany left and how she stayed with him while he did art work and moved from job to job, but how she couldn't stay when he found the Lord. "I didn't think she would really leave," he says.

How could he have been so stupid? The whole valley was on her side. Even my mom said, "How can he think God will provide? The Lord helps those who help themselves." I look at Janice who's smiling, swallowing every word.

"It was hard, knowing people were saying I didn't care about my family," Arlyn says. "I had to trust that God knew I

90

would send support when I got on my feet and would visit the kids whenever I could." His voice gets real soft and I'm afraid he might cry. But he bucks up. "That was thirty-five years ago. But sometimes I still wake in the night and listen for the kids. And I want to hold that woman I loved to touch and make love to."

I scoot down in my chair. Why the hell does he have to talk like that?

"When that happens, I have a moment of bitterness," he says. "Then I pray for God to make me thankful for my blessings."

I glance at Terrill to see the smirk. But he's hiding it.

"I want to unburden myself from that hurt. Would you pray for me Francoise?"

She nods. "God, please help Arlyn have peace of mind. Help him empty his heart of bitterness. Bring him comfort. In Jesus's name. Amen."

Everybody knows how to do this. I wonder if Arlyn feels unburdened. Doesn't he know people think he's a fool?

Then one by one they tell their worries. Terrill says his wife Sage is still scared about his logging alone. He feels bad because she agreed to stay in the valley because of him. But he loves the eerie whine of alder tops rubbing together and the hoot of owls. He says, "You'd never hear those things with the whistle blasting and the cat revving up."

My old man called Terrill a moron. "Who logs with mules?" he said. "And alone?" I'm glad he isn't here. "Hobnobbing with crazies," he'd say. "Going soft in the head."

Arlyn tells Terrill to assure Sage, "His eye is on the sparrow."

Terrill smiles. "God would have to be pretty busy to watch everything. Sometimes things just happen." He's right about that. Uncle John was on a crew and still a vine maple got him.

Francoise says, "It's not because God isn't watching."

Terrill nods and says he thinks God's in everything—trees and animals and people—not really personal but more of a presence tying things together. He says, "But the presence can't stop something bad from happening."

"Won't, not can't," Francoise says. "Man has free agency and is responsible for his actions." I figure she's talking about me. Then she says, "It's people who start wars." She sounds sure, like she did when she taught that one plus one *had* to equal two. Even though I hate being here, it's nice to know that not everybody agrees about God.

I look at Terrill, waiting for him to roll his eyes or make a face at Francoise. But he's a good faker. He smiles at Francoise and says again that he feels bad for Sage. He asks Janice to pray for him which she does, making it up on the spot, like it's easy.

Francoise goes next, talking about Darla's studying in Greece this summer. She says "She's looking forward to it. But after Turkey's invasion last year...well, I think things could flare up again. Why can't she choose a safer place?"

I guess Francoise thinks God *could* watch out for Darla if he wanted to, but since Darla has free agency, whatever that is, and is walking into a hornet's nest, it'll be her own fault if anything goes wrong. Or something like that.

I look at my watch. Minutes are crawling along, slow as prison time. My stomach jumps when Janice says, "I'll go next" and takes my hand. I wonder if she's just nervous or plans to say something shocking.

She sighs. "My mom's so negative," she says. "I wish she wouldn't see the bad side of things. I dread her calls because I know she'll talk about the problems we're going to run into." I'm glad to hear Janice isn't mad at me, but I don't like thinking she isn't as calm about moving here as she lets on. What if her mother talks her into thinking I'm a no-good failure?

I take a slow deep breath. Why can't people just leave each other alone? Janice's mother is like Paula, always looking at the bad side. Paula kept telling me I wasn't making enough in my dad's store. She said that before we were married, she thought I would be more of a go-getter. Why couldn't we move to the city? She was sick of smelling like grain and feed and hay.

At the trial, the lawyer asked me why I wasn't more supportive. He said several of her friends knew she was depressed.

"I tried to hug her," I told the court.

"Is that *all* you did, Mr. Mullins?" I didn't know what to say. If someone doesn't want to be hugged, what can you do? I couldn't say in front of people that I told her I loved her, but it didn't help, especially when she was pregnant. I couldn't say, if I accidentally bumped her breasts in the night, she snapped, "Don't you know how sore they are?" Once she said, "These boobs make me look like a cow." When I said I thought she was beautiful, she told me to shut up.

How could I say in a courtroom that she asked me once, "How would you like to have something enormous hanging out in front of you?" I laughed and said, "I do," something that would have made her laugh when we dated." But she said, "You wish," stomped off to the bedroom and slammed the door.

After Terrill prays for Janice, she squeezes my hand. I don't squeeze back. I breathe in and out real slow a few times to calm myself down. Then this story called 'The Telltale Heart' I read in Junior English leaps into my mind. It's about this murderer whose heart pounds so loud it gives him away.

What if Francoise and Arlyn and Terrill and Janice find out how mad I was at Paula that day? She was yelling at me, "You're boring. All you talk about is how much feed you sell. Who the hell cares? How did I know you were just a Daddy's boy?"

I hated her at that moment and I couldn't think right. I yelled at her, "God damn you. I wish you'd never got pregnant. You'll be a lousy mother."

She started screaming, "I knew you didn't want this baby. I don't know why I thought I'd want to be with you." And she reached to the mantle and grabbed the gun she said she bought to protect herself when I worked late. She pointed it at her belly, then twirled it like a toy. She got a sneer on her mouth that got bigger and bigger and bigger.

I lunged for her. I couldn't think about how I used to love her. I just couldn't stand her yelling and sneering at me. And then I grabbed for the gun and it went off. At first I felt glad when she shut up, but then I saw the blood and that awful terror on her face.

I know I'm not a good person; good people don't have that kind of accident no matter what my lawyer said. Arlyn can talk all he wants about people getting rid of their burdens but these people don't know what burdens are. Confessions might be good for the soul, but they aren't good for the heart. A heart you stopped.

Janice squeezes my hand again. She can't expect me to make a fool of myself in front of this little hippie. But she stood up to her mother and moved to the valley. I think of my mother who would say I should be grateful to God.

I let go of Janice's hand and cross my arms over my chest. My head's about to split open.

If I can just hang on a little longer and keep from being weak and spilling my guts in front of Francois and crazy Arlyn and the hippie.

"You all right?" Janice whispers.

I hug my chest tighter and see out of the corner of my eye she's signaling Arlyn with a head shake. She's willing to let me off the hook, and I don't have the guts to make her happy by coming up with some little confession. "Keep your mouth shut," I tell myself. "You'll be sorry if you say a thing. Just hang on a little longer."

"Let's rise and join hands," Arlyn says. "If no one else decides to share, I'll offer a closing prayer." He's trying to smoke me out. Terrill on my left and Janice on my right wait while I unfold my arms, then take my hands. I don't like holding a man's hand. A wimp man at that. The only time I ever held a guy's hand was in football and just until we said, "Let's go."

Arlyn's waiting just a minute. I've almost made it. I look around for something to fix my eyes on and spot that enormous beam, holding up the room. I stare into the wood, pretending

I'm burrowing between the rings inch by inch. The smell of cedar pulls me toward the core. Farther and farther away from everybody. Deeper and deeper. The wood's dense and tinder dry. I take a deep breath but choke on the fibers. They sting my throat. I try again but only breathe fibers. I try to slither out the way I came. This dry old wood is drinking my sweat, squashing me, holding me tight. I jerk hard to get free of the crushing tons, but I'm stuck. Trapped. Caught. Can't get out. Wife killer! Baby killer! In big time trouble. Accident? Come on man, who am I shittin'?

"It *was* an accident."

Janice pats my arm. "It's okay, hon. We know…"

"It was an accident, but I wanted her to shut up." My voice is angry and loud.

Someone gasps. Maybe Francoise. Maybe Janice. I can breathe again, but then everything is quiet and I know it's all over. Everybody in the valley will know by morning. I'll never be able to face anybody, and nobody will come to the store.

Even Arlyn looks bug-eyed for a minute. Then he says, "Uh, let's ask God to be with our brother, Lanny," and prays for love and forgiveness and all that heavy stuff that makes my sin seem so awful it has to be forgiven in front of everybody.

Francoise clears her throat. Janice lets go of my hand and digs in her purse, then blows her nose. Like my old man said, you're a damn fool if you trust anybody. They either humiliate you with a stupid prayer or drop your hand. Or the crazy hippie on your left wraps his hands around yours like a baseball glove, making it hard to pull away.

A Tale of the Whiskey Man

Darla

1952

I'd never walked it alone, but I wasn't afraid. All I knew when Mother said, "Darla, I need another egg for my cake. You'll have to run to the store," was that this was my chance.

"I'm ready," I told her. My cat Billy and I had explored every inch of our five acres. Sometimes we were fishermen, scooping crawdads from the creek to feed gold miners, heading to California; sometimes I picked black berries while Billy—a ferocious cougar—was on look-out for black bears. The most exciting thing we'd encountered that spring was a strange rustling in the woods at the back of the pasture. I told Billy it might be a Japanese incendiary balloon left from the war that Mother had talked about. He wasn't worried, but I grabbed him and hid behind a Canadian thistle. We'd waited for an explosion but nothing happened.

I loved roaming with Billy, but I longed for new territory. I figured if I returned quickly with the eggs intact, Mother may let me walk the extra mile past the store to where Uncle Murry would take me fossil hunting in the river.

We lived on the highway, a quarter mile and around a bend from the valley store. Though it was sunny, the air was crisp.

Before I reached the door, Mother held out the navy blue sweater Grandma Jenkins knitted for me and waited while I pushed my arms down the sleeves. It was bulky, with sleeves so long that, when I played in the creek, they unrolled and got dripping wet.

"It's colder than it looks," Mother said, buttoned the sweater and handed me a cap.

"Do I have to?" I said, taking the hat but not putting it on. "It heats up my head."

She tucked the hat into my pocket. "But if you feel cold, put it on. It's better to be..."

"Safe than sorry."

"You know me too well," she said, then handed me a slip of paper that read: "One dozen eggs. Please charge to our account. Françoise." Then she said, "Give the note to Julia and she'll take care of it. And don't dawdle. I need the eggs for tonight's dessert. Chiffon cakes are fragile."

I opened the door and stepped onto the porch, waiting for the door to close behind me, but she followed me out. "Remember what I've told you," she said. "Look both ways when you cross the highway. Those logging trucks..."

"Don't stop for anyone," I said, and hurried down the front steps. It's a warning I'd passed on to Billy. If I caught him sneaking to the end of the drive or stretching his neck toward the schoolyard across the road, I called him back. If he didn't budge, I carried him to the back of the house and reminded him about Cuddles, my big yellow cat who Carl, my stepfather, found dead by the highway two years ago. Carl said it was a cat's nature to wander and that he'd died, roaming free, but I missed him something awful. Before Billy showed up, I had to play crawdads and pioneers and bear thieves by myself. It wasn't the same.

On that spring day, with eggs as my mission, I waved at my mother, then checked the yard to make sure Billy hadn't spotted me and would try to follow. When he didn't show up, I hurried down the sidewalk where I unlatched the gate, slipped through, then latched it behind me. At the road, I listened for shifting gears, then looked to the right, to the left, back and forth to be absolutely sure. Unfortunately, old Rhodie Sherman only looked one way, a tragedy Mother reminded me of if she thought I wasn't listening. And she would be watching from the window.

Once across the road, I passed the schoolyard, the one place beyond our fence where I was allowed to play, and didn't slow—even a little—at the barn that last year's snow had caved in. When I'd asked if I could go inside, just once, Mother said, "When you're older. There could be a pitchfork or baling wire in the hay." But Carl had given it one more year to collapse. So I doubted I'd ever see from inside how the ceiling looked, pointing down.

When I reached the bridge and culvert that crossed the creek, I skipped quickly across. In flood time, the creek rose nearly to the top and once had spilled over the road. But in the summer it was a trickle. The August before, when Liz Martin had come to the valley for a visit, her Aunt Doris sent us to the store. On the way, we climbed down the bank into the culvert.

"It's kind of dark in..." I started to say, but stopped when my words echoed. I shivered, then spotted the pile of sticks someone had lit for a fire and an old blanket thrown to the side.

"What's that?" I whispered to Liz who was kicking the ashes with her toe.

"Maybe kidnappers," Liz said and told me about the Lindbergh baby.

I thought she must be kidding, but when a car rumbled overhead and the culvert rattled, I ran out of the darkness and climbed the bank. We promised to keep the campfire a secret. And though I knew there couldn't be kidnappers in Timber, I'd skipped fast across the bridge ever since.

On the store porch I cleared my throat and stood as straight as I could. When I walked in, Richard was standing by the stove and nodded hello. Harriet, the aunt we never visited, was looking at work gloves. "Are you traveling alone, today?" Richard asked when I stepped up to the counter. I nodded and felt proud. The

Websters had bought the store a few months before, but they'd never seen me there by myself.

"We have a customer," Richard said to Julia, who slid a bookmarker into her novel and set it on the cash register. I saw it was *Of Mice and Men* and wondered why she was reading a children's book. Richard unlatched the door of the stove and threw in another chunk of wood.

"I see that we do," Julia said and smiled at me. Her voice was soft but serious. I couldn't help staring at her short blond hair, combed nice and neat around her face, and the little earrings that matched the black and orange squares in her blouse.

"May I help you?"

I liked it that she asked the question in the grown-up voice she used with Richard, and I tucked Mother's note back into my pocket. "One dozen..." But before I could finish, Harriet said,

"Are there anymore gloves in the back? Sim needs a bigger size."

"I think those are the only ones we have," Richard said, closing the stove door and walking toward the counter. "Julia will check."

"I'm helping a customer," Julia said, not taking her eyes from me.

I opened my mouth to continue, but Richard said, "Excuse me a moment, honey." He whispered to Julia something about a chip and Harriet's shoulder but stopped when she walked toward the counter.

"Oh," Harriet said when she saw me. "I didn't know you had another customer." She nodded at me and I noticed how different she looked from Julia. Harriet's voice was deep, and she wore a blue-and-red flannel shirt that hung loose around her. Her brown hair was pulled back and held with a clip. And her nose was sharp.

"Hello," I said, wishing my voice sounded louder.

"That's all right," Richard said. "I'll take care of this young lady, and Julia will help you."

Julia's face turned red and I wondered if she felt embarrassed, knowing Richard had talked about my aunt in front of me. Maybe she'd figured out what Mother said about this valley, that talking about people unless it's in your own home wasn't safe. I wished she knew I could keep a secret. Or maybe she was upset, having to switch customers. Whatever she felt, she said calmly to me, "I'm sorry. Richard will help you."

"The largest ones are too big for me but too small for Sim," Harriet said and held the pair out to Julia as they walked toward the shelf of work gloves and shirts. I was so busy watching them that I jumped when Richard said, "Now young lady. What can I do for you?" He leaned on the counter toward me.

I reached in my pocket for the note and handed it to him. Then I cleared my throat. "I would like a dozen eggs," I said, making my voice firm, the way Mother asked for things.

He folded the note and handed it back. "Can you carry those home yourself?"

I was getting ready to say that I could, when Harriet, who was waiting for Julia to return from the back room, blurted out, "I was hauling loads of wood when I was her age."

Richard nodded at me, as if he'd not heard Harriet, but I could see his jaw tighten. "It'll take me a few minutes to candle a dozen," he said. "I'll be right back."

I knew Mother would have reminded him kindly that she was in a hurry, but I didn't think of it fast enough. I just stood very still, not slouching or leaning on the counter, and thought about Mother, glancing at the clock every few minutes.

To take my mind off the cake, I read Leo Martin's 'poem'. Liz said her Aunt Doris printed the words and told the store owners it belonged above the door. Sometimes Carl recited it and said Leo had hit the nail on the head.

These doors are really famous, though one would hardly think it so,
They have swung for generations, as folks they come and go,
They have weathered grave disasters—fires, floods and quakes,

But they never have ceased their swinging and they
still have what it takes.
They have let the people in and out through half a
dozen wars,
And still the best people in the world pass through
these doors.

I wondered who was best—Harriet, Julia, Richard? Mother
said Harriet would argue with the devil himself. Yet she'd just
stuck up for me; Richard was candling my eggs, but he'd made
Julia switch customers. I liked Julia best, but did that mean she
was best? And if someone was best, who was worst?

When Richard finished candling, he set the carton of eggs
on the counter. He was just pulling down our tab that sat in a
metal tray in a bank of trays by the cash register, when Nathan
Mullins burst in. "I'm sorry to bother you," he said to Richard,
"but this is an emergency. We've run out of fuel oil and Dad's
got pneumonia. How long before I can get some?" He had dark
circles under his eyes and a scraggly beard.

Richard smiled at him. "I can help you right now," he said
and handed our tab to Julia who had just reached the counter
with Harriet behind her. Harriet stopped every few steps to
frown at the gloves' stitching and lining.

"We found a pair," Julia said to him but took the tab he
handed her.

"Nathan's father has pneumonia," he told her. "He needs
fuel oil quickly."

I watched her face turn red again, but she calmly said to
Harriet who had dropped the gloves on the counter. "I'll help you
in a minute. Richard has an emergency." Then she wrote "Eggs,
twenty-five cents," on our tab and held it out for me to see.

When I nodded, Julia set the box of eggs in a sack and
pushed it halfway across the counter. But then she pulled it back
and lifted the eggs out of the bag. "These aren't the easiest things
to carry," she said. "And you have quite a trek ahead of you."

"She's a big girl," Harriet said.

"She certainly is," Julia said and looked directly at Harriet, who didn't step back but lifted the gloves off the counter. Julia was brave. Most people didn't argue with Harriet. "When I was just younger than Darla," Julia said, "I broke a carton of eggs. And my mother was very upset." She smiled. I stared at her. How could someone so perfect have ever been in trouble? "It's true that I was swinging the bag a little. But it's also true the clerk hadn't secured it properly."

"Hm," Harriet said.

Julia opened a drawer and pulled out a large rubber band. "I don't want the same thing to happen to you," she said in her gentle voice, as she returned the eggs to a smaller bag, folded the top down several times and stretched the rubber band around the whole package. She slid it across the counter. "There you go," she said. "And I'll look forward to seeing you again soon."

"Thank you," I said, lifted the bag and held it carefully then nodded to Harriet who almost smiled.

On the store porch, I climbed down the steps carefully. After all the care Julia had taken, I didn't want to let her down. Then I stayed on the store side of the road as Mother had drilled into me. I felt relief I didn't have to cross the road again.

Just before I reached the bridge, I stopped a moment and shifted the eggs to my other arm. It was hard to carry them firmly but not too firmly. As I started up again, I sang the words of the store poem to the tune of "Sweetly Sings the Donkey." "These doors are really famous/de dum, de dum, de dum."

At the "Eee Haw, Eee Haw" part, I brayed and laughed out loud as I sped up. I would sing the song to Billy when I got home but soften the braying. Loud noises scared him.

I hurried across the bridge and was just repeating the "Eee Haw's" for the third time when I saw a man ahead of me. He swayed like he was dizzy which slowed him down. Sometimes he stopped completely. What was wrong? Even though my house was around the bend and out of sight, I wasn't far from home.

When I caught up to him, I nodded politely, the way Mother had taught me to do with my elders. He was a small man, about five feet five like Uncle Murry, and I couldn't tell if he was Carl's or Grandpa Jenkins' age. His face didn't look old, but Grandpa Jenkins, who used a cane, wobbled in the same way. This man wore a wrinkled shirt, the kind Mother would have made Carl put in the ironing basket. I couldn't say, "Hello Mr. Martin or Uncle Murry or Mr. Hekula" as Mother would want me to, for I'd never seen him. So I just nodded again and said, "Hello," as I started to pass.

But instead of nodding, he said, "Hey, where you going in such a hurry, little girl? Where you going, huh?"

"Home," I said and kept walking.

But he reached out and grabbed for my arm. "Hold up there," he said and staggered faster, trying to catch up as I kept walking. I knew mother would be getting worried about the eggs, but I didn't want to be rude. I stopped a minute, then turned and walked back toward him a few steps, and faced home again when he was beside me. He smelled different than anyone I'd known, and up close I saw his eyes were puffy and dark.

"That's a good girl," he said. "Now where could you be going in such a hurry?"

"Home," I said again and pointed around the bend. "My mother's waiting..."

"Live in this burg long?" he said, slowing even more, as we came to where the shoulder dropped into a ditch, then rose to the sagging barn.

"My father has," I said, and paused as I heard the mill whistle that meant it was the end of the shift. Most of the men would be heading home, but Carl would stay late to change gang saws. He would be home in an hour, and Mother still had to bake the cake and fix dinner.

"I have to hurry," I said, but the man, barely shuffling now, spread his legs farther apart to keep his balance.

"Who's your father?"

"Carl Tarbell," I said, shifting the eggs to the other arm. "Well, he's really my stepfather. My real father died in Pearl Harbor. But I never knew him."

"Carl Tarbell? Went to school with him. Nice fellow. Helped people all the time."

I nodded. That was Carl all right. Once, during a windstorm, he'd left the house at three in the morning to help Leo Martin rush Doris to the hospital.

"What's your name?" I said, knowing Carl would ask.

"Oh, he wouldn't remember me. I only went to school here a few weeks. Yup, he helped people all the time. I'll bet you help people too," he said. "I left something in that barn, but I need a hand, getting down that bank."

"I have to get home," I said, trying to hurry, but he swayed toward me and fell against my shoulder. I braced myself, as it was the arm with the eggs. While I shifted them to the other arm, he gripped my shoulder, and I was surprised how strong he was.

"Come on," he said. "I have to get something in the barn." Then he took a step toward the ditch, pulling me with him.

I could see our front fence now and tried to pull away, but he dragged me after him.

"If you just wait a minute, I'll take the eggs to my mother, then come back to..." I was saying when I noticed Billy, squeezing under the gate. Then as the man was tugging me down into the ditch, I heard the shifting gears and saw Arlyn's truck. And then Billy, running into the highway, across one lane and disappearing under the wheels.

I pulled against the man's grip, my heart pounding, terrified of the lump of fur I'd see like what happened with Cuddles.

But when Arlyn's truck rolled by, there was no lump, just Billy, frozen to the spot. "Billy," I screamed, yanking myself free and dropping the eggs in the process. Then without looking left or right, I darted toward him.

Little did I know that Mother had stepped onto the porch just in time to see me dash into the road, scoop Billy up and hug him so tightly he squirmed; just in time to see Harriet swerve to avoid me, then screech to a halt in front of our house.

Harriet and I, the bag of broken eggs I'd picked up in one hand and the squirming Billy in the other, arrived at our front gate together.

"You ran across the road without looking," Mother said at the same time I was saying, "Arlyn almost hit Billy, and I hurried as fast as I could, except the man..."

"What man?" Harriet blurted out. Mother frowned.

"The sick man who couldn't stand..."

"That's why I'm here," Harriet said. "Julia wanted me to check on Darla because of the man Joe Mullins saw staggering down the road." Then she turned to me. "Where is he?" she said with a voice that made me take a step backwards.

I lifted the arm with the egg bag hanging from it, in the direction of the barn and held onto Billy even tighter with the other. "He said he needed help getting to the barn and was..."

"Don't you know you can't trust strangers?" Harriet said, then ran out the gate, stood on her tiptoes, and shielded her eyes to see into the field toward the barn. After several seconds, she shook her head. "I'll have Sim come back and look for him."

I didn't know why she was so upset or why Mother yelled "Thank you so much, Harriet. I'll call you." Then Mother led me through the garage, where I made her close the door before letting go of Billy, and into the kitchen where she sat me at the table.

She took the sack of eggs and set it on the counter.

"I was really careful with them until I had to drop them," I said but it didn't seem to matter.

She frowned at me. "Aunt Harriet's right. You have to be careful of strangers," she said.

"He knew Carl."

"Besides that," she said, as if she didn't hear me, "You ran out in the road without looking."

"Only because Billy ran in front of Arlyn's truck," I said. "And Arlyn didn't stop."

"I'm sure he didn't see Billy. And what if he'd hit you?"

"I'll look both ways after this. I promise."

Mother hugged me so tight, I couldn't breathe inside Grandma Jenkins' sweater. "I think it's best if you don't go across to the school yard for a few days, just to give us a chance to think about things," she said.

"What things?" I said, pulling away.

"Just things, honey," she said.

I could tell there was no use arguing, so I went to the garage to talk to Billy. I told him how disappointed I was as I loved playing on the monkey bars and swinging on the swings in the schoolyard. And I wondered how long it'd be before Mother would let me go to the store again. I didn't feel like singing "These Doors," to Billy but told him I'd sing it later.

When Mother called me into the house, Billy waited by the garage door for me to let him out. But I reminded him he'd run across the road and thought it best he stay in for a few nights to think things over. When he wondered, "what things?" I couldn't explain. I only knew whatever they were, people seemed scared of them. And they spoiled your plans.

A Winner

Leo

1976

When I break the news to Doris, she's tenderizing steaks. "How would you like to see Vincent Price?" I say, watching her face. She's not easy to impress.

She stops pounding and peers over her glasses. "*The* Vincent Price?"

I hold Edie Lou's letter above the hammer. "It's that poetry contest. The winner gets to recite his poem at a conference in August and meets Vincent Price."

She rests the hammer on the steak then reads aloud, "Leo, a **Big Congratulations.** America's Poetry Society judges have chosen you out of hundreds of poets as one of five finalists for your entry, 'Steam Donkey Logging.' Please join us. Edie Lou Porter."

"My word," she says, picking up the hammer and smacking the steak, hard. "Couldn't they just send you the prize?"

"You have to be there to win. I know I don't have a chance. But it'd be nice to go."

She nods as she sprinkles the steaks with flour.

"We've never been to Florida," I tell her. "And we'd have three weeks to get ready."

"It's four thousand miles and hot in August," she says arranging the steaks in the skillet.

"I suppose. I fold the letter and slip it into my pocket. "I'm going out to cut Ragwort. They're coming back thick."

In the orchard, I snip the yellow flowers that choke the life out of things. As I stack them for the burn barrel, I think about my seventy-second birthday in two weeks. How did I get so old? Going to Florida would be something unusual. Even if I didn't win, *The Valley News* would write about my trip.

It's not that people don't know I write poetry. Sometimes at the annual Pioneer meeting, I'm asked to recite one. Afterwards someone always says, "Leo, you've got it down just how it was with drag saws and whistle punks and puncheon roads." But that's as far as it goes. The editor from *Logger's World* who published my "Logging in the Thirties," said years from now my poems might be the only way people will know how we used to log—with steam donkeys and spar trees. But Doris is the only one who knows he said that, and she's not interested in logging.

A few days later, when I walk into the house for lunch, Doris' face is flushed. "Whew, it's hot," she says, pulling off her sweater and throwing it over a chair.

"Are you all right?" I say and start unlacing my boots, heavy with mud from the creek. I've been balancing my water wheel paddles.

"Just tired. You know, we're not getting any younger."

"I know. Not much time left to accomplish something."

"Good heavens," she says and opens the dishwasher. "You've only been out of the woods two years and you've fixed the plumbing and re-roofed the shop. And you help everybody who comes along. What more do you want to accomplish?"

I think of saying, "Something to be remembered by," but after my bout with prostate cancer, she'll worry I'm hiding something. "Something out of the ordinary."

She stares at me, then shakes her head. "What about a blue ribbon for figuring the board feet in Carl's load just by looking at it. Nobody but cousin Hank came close."

"That was only a logging show."

She opens the silverware drawer. "Well, how about John Mullins. Isn't hauling a man two miles through the woods, after he's been smashed in the head with a vine maple, important? What else do you need to accomplish?" She sounds irritated. "You can finally relax."

"I'm not sure," I say and walk into the living room. Maybe it'd be different if we had kids. But after Doris' four miscarriages, it wasn't worth trying again.

I'm surprised Doris isn't restless. Before her heart trouble, she was full steam ahead. The first time I saw her, she was dressed as Friar Tuck, emceeing the annual Timber program where we raise money for cemetery upkeep and the four highway lights. She was Master of the Grange for five years and every year donated a quilt to be auctioned off at its charity drive. Her heart surgeries changed everything. Now, she does whatever she can and lets the rest go.

But I want to do something that changes things. Like what happened to Francoise. At the last Grange meeting she told me she just got a letter from a student she taught twenty years ago who said he passed onto his kids the stories he learned in her Oregon History class about Lewis and Clark and the Bridge of the Gods and Chief Multnomah. And he doesn't even live in Oregon anymore. Those stories will be alive long after Francoise is gone.

I pull Edie Lou's letter out of my pocket and read, "The Festival's only forty-five minutes from Disney World. Make your reservations today so you don't miss this chance of a lifetime."

Doris walks in before I can put the letter away. "You don't have to win a contest to be important," she says. "Everybody around here says nobody knows the woods like you do."

"Around here."

"What about Liz? She knows about your logging and she's in Los Angeles."

"I guess so," I say but know our niece hasn't taken one thing about the woods with her. The summers she stayed with us, I showed her how to name trees by their bark and color and needles. But to this day, she can't tell a spruce from a fir.

Doris slowly crosses the room and sits in her rocker close to where I'm standing in front of the window. She raises her legs, one at a time, onto the footstool. The doctor told her whenever she can to elevate her feet. She looks serious. "Leo, you've lived in this valley all your life, and the few times we've traveled, we've gone together. I don't think the doctor will let me fly, and even if he says yes, I couldn't take that Florida heat. You would have to go by yourself."

Her voice is calm, but she's tapping out a worry signal on the rocker arm. "What if you got lost on your way back to the hotel or out to the cabs or somewhere?" She begins rocking.

I know she's thinking about our trip to Liz's. We took a walk and went about six blocks when Doris said we should go back, as she hadn't brought Liz's address. I said all we had to do was return the way we came and started off. But Doris insisted we go the opposite direction.

Sure enough, just when I was ready to say we should turn back, there we were, at Liz's apartment. Doris chided me about that one. "How you can find your way around the woods with no roads and a bunch of trees but get lost in six blocks with signs everywhere is beyond me."

"These buildings all look the same," I told her. "And there's so much noise, you can't think." The streets and buildings in Florida would most likely be like that.

"I probably wouldn't win anyway," I tell her and stuff the letter back in the envelope.

"That's not the point," she says, then rocks to her feet. I watch her walk toward the kitchen, like she's slogging through mud.

Later that afternoon, when Doris is taking a nap, I find my money belt in the spare room. I unzip the pocket to see if it would hold Edie Lou's tiny map of Orlando. The army material would be hot in Florida. Then I go to the den and look up Continental Airline's number so it'll be handy in case I decide to go.

As I write it on Edie Lou's letter, I feel uneasy. The only time I've made business plans long distance was ten years ago. Doris said I was always inventing something, then feeling frustrated when a year or so later someone patented something similar. She suggested I call one of those companies in Portland to see what they thought about the hook I was working on.

"You're better on the phone than I am," I told her after I settled on Samuals and Sons. I liked the idea of a family business.

"I wouldn't know how to explain your invention," she said. "It'll be good practice."

I didn't ask, "Practice for what?" Doris wasn't one to pull punches about her health. So I dialed, and a woman said, "Samuals and Sons Invention Searchers."

"I made a slack chain hook," I said. "It's not like anything I've seen and I want..."

"I don't talk about the inventions," she said.

"Can I talk to Samuals then?"

"There isn't any Samuals. It's Garrison and Lawrence. Hold the line, please." Five minutes later she came back. "Mr. Garrison is tied up. You want to hold?"

"I'm in Timber," I said. "This is long distance."

She was quiet. I thought we'd been cut off until she repeated, "Do you want to hold?" She sounded annoyed.

"Could he call me back? You see this slack chain hook hasn't been made and..."

"I don't talk about the inventions. I just transfer the calls. What's your number?"

"429-3894."

She sighed. "Area code first," she said. "I need your area code first."

The next day when Garrison called, I described the hook. He said, "I think you have something. There's certainly a market for logging equipment in this part of the country."

Then he told me to send three hundred dollars for the initial search fee and we were on our way.

"That's a lot, just to look up a few things, isn't it?" Doris said when I hung up.

"He thinks I have something," I told her. "And Carl Tarbell said I needed to get a patent on it fast, that it's the handiest thing to take up slack he's ever used."

"I suppose," Doris said, "but why don't you check with the Better Business Bureau first."

I didn't want to make another call. So the next day I sent the money. Two months later Garrison wrote saying there were similar patents and sent a page of their pictures. But he said if I sent two hundred more, they'd be glad to do more research. I could tell mine was simpler to use and easier to make and cheaper to fix. I didn't like the idea of sending more money but would have if Doris hadn't been upset. She said it sounded like the shysters *Sixty Minutes* warned against. They pull you in deeper and deeper, and all you get out of it is a big bill.

I dropped it after that but still look at that hook in my shop and make a few for people who've heard about it. Before I found out I was a finalist in this poetry contest, I wondered if that hook was my one chance to do something important.

At midnight, about ten days after I get the letter, Doris sits straight up in bed and switches on the lamp. "Leo are you awake," she whispers.

I don't tell her I've been staring at the ceiling, wondering how close the hotel is to the Convention Center and if the shirt Liz gave me for Christmas will be cool enough for Florida.

She cuddles up close to me, the way she does when she's nervous. I lay my cheek against her hair. After all these years, I still like the softness of it.

"I had an awful dream," she says. "You were in Florida, saying your poem to a big audience and when you finished, you couldn't find your way off the stage. People swarmed around, like they wanted to help, but one boy grabbed your wallet and a taxi driver stopped but drove off when you opened the door to get in." She rolls over and faces me. "You've never even caught a cab."

"In Los Angeles."

"You rode in one, but Liz made the call and paid the bill and knew what to tip."

"The convention's two miles from the hotel. I could walk if I had to."

"In a strange city?" I feel her shudder. "That dream put me in a cold sweat. I thought I'd never see you again." She gets up for a glass of water.

When she comes back, she says, "Let's call Liz." She turns the clock toward her, then picks up the receiver.

"It's too late."

"Liz is a night person. It'll be all right."

"Liz doesn't know anything about Florida," I say but don't tell her that last summer I showed Liz the entry materials and the poem I was sending. She agreed it was better than Lily May Redfield's 'Ode to a Southern Town,' that won the year before. But she didn't seem excited about it. Liz likes poems that don't rhyme. Once when she was in college, she showed me a poem she was reading for her English class that said nothing ran through the universe and everyone had to endure nothing and everything came to nothing. It was the most negative thing I ever read. When she asked what I thought of it, I told her, "It seems like it's about nothing." She said "Exactly, and that's what makes it so meaningful."

"I don't want to call Liz," I tell Doris. She hesitates, then hangs up.

"I hope you're not thinking this Edie Lou Porter is doing you a favor by choosing your poem," she says. "She's in it for the money."

"I know, but people like Vincent Price don't come cheap."

"This is a business for her—all those five-dollar entry fees..."

I don't want to admit it's ten and suddenly feel heavy in my rib cage and chest, the way I did when I was pinned under an alder.

"Let's face it; that woman's making a bundle," she says.

"So is the light company," I tell her and point toward the lamp.

Doris flicks it off, rolls away from me and lets out a big sigh.

"Everything will be okay. Go back to sleep," I say. But I don't fall asleep for a long time. Doris may be right about Edie Lou, but that doesn't matter. I picture myself on that stage, take a deep breath and recite to myself, "The faller shouted 'timber,' and the eighty tons, set free, crashed headlong down the canyon raising havoc and debris. The hooker bellowed 'Puncher, raise the pressure,' through the din. 'Screw the pop valve to three-sixty or we'll never pull her in.'" All those people, listening to me and finally knowing what it means to be a logger.

The next morning, before Doris is up, I go to the den and write the Regency to save me a room. Then I drive to the Valley Store and mail the letter. When I return, Doris is sitting at the kitchen table drinking coffee and taking her heart pills. She's set out my cup.

I pour myself coffee and sip it as I walk around the kitchen. "Why are you pacing?" she says. "Sit down."

I pull out my chair and swish my coffee around. Then I clear my throat. "I'm really thinking about going."

She looks at me, then points to the morning paper. "Some strange disease swept through this American Legion Convention."

I glance at the headline. "Philadelphia's a long way from Florida."

"The point is that it came out of nowhere, and people have died from it." She clanks her cup as she sets it in the saucer. "After your cancer scare, I think you're pushing your luck."

"I'll be all right." I smile at her, but she doesn't smile back. I turn my chair so I can look out onto the porch and continue sipping my coffee.

"You know, Leo," she says, "every morning for forty-five years when you left for the woods, I was scared you would get in the way of a chainsaw or a widow maker or a D9 or a snapped haul back or who knows what."

I'm surprised she knows any of those names.

"And after you get through all that, now you want to wander around in Florida."

"It's five hundred for first place."

"But I still don't see if they're on the up and up, why they can't just send it. And after your hotel and plane costs, you wouldn't clear much." She carries her cup to the sink. The skin on her face looks smooth, but I know the surgery scars under her robe.

"Don't worry," I tell her.

"That's easier said than done," she says and starts rinsing the dishes. I was planning to call Continental, but I have another day so decide to go to my shop to finish sharpening Carl's saw. He's building Francoise a wishing well. As I slide the blade into the carriage, I think about Doris, worrying about me all those years. Then I tighten the clamps and bevel each tooth to a twenty-degree hook and twenty-five degree cutting angle. I want it to do a good job for him.

Later when Carl stops by, he orders more hooks for friends who've seen his. "When you going to get a patent on those things?" he says. "They'd sell like crazy."

"It's been ten years since those patent people said there were others like it. Who knows what they have now."

"Those guys don't know the woods," he says, turning the hook over in his hands.

We're quiet a minute. "You know, I'm thinking about going to Florida," I tell him.

"Really? I hear it's hot this year."

"I'm a finalist in a poetry contest. And Vincent Price will be there."

"*The* Vincent Price?"

I nod. "Not that I'd win."

"You never know," he says. "You've sure come a long way from those logging ditties my dad said you use to recite in the bunk house."

"In '32."

"He said there was a guy from Alaska who'd say, 'What you have for us tonight, Leo?'"

"Harvey Schultz."

"Dad said you always came up with something."

"There was a lot to make up a poem about back then. Like the time your dad was up a hundred-twenty foot spar and dropped a lit cigar down his pants or when the whistle punk fouled up the signals and the loader dropped a two-hundred foot cedar on the cab. And then there was that day I saw a spruce sticking out of a fir."

"Things sure have changed," Carl says and turns to walk to his pickup. But then he turns back. "You know, day before yesterday, I saw quite a sight." Then he says I should head up the Burn Hill Road by Lydia's, pass the Oakdale Lumber Company's stand of second growth, keep going three hundred yards along Arlyn's South line and down into Mullins' canyon. "It's about a mile past where Hank Hekula saw the bear cubs," he says.

"I know the place."

"There's an old growth that has the darndest bulge you ever saw, a couple hundred feet up. I don't know what it is, but the tree's grown around it and kept going."

"The dickens. I thought they logged that out in the thirties."

"Probably so many straight ones, they didn't need to cut something deformed. But it'll go next time. Enough second growth in there now, they'll clear cut in a year or two." Carl hoists the saw over his shoulder, and I walk him to the pickup. "Better go to Florida," Carl says as he latches the tailgate. "We're not getting any younger."

"Carl says we're not getting any younger," I tell Doris when I go in for dinner. "He ordered four more hooks."

"Oh?" she says as she scrubs a radish.

"He says those patent guys don't know a thing about logging and that these hooks are still the best things around."

She scrubs the radish so hard the red's coming off. "Nobody's keeping you from sending in more money and trying to get a patent," she says. "But the Better Business..."

"I'm just saying Carl thinks I had something is all."

She stands stone still for a few moments, staring out the window and across the pasture that leads into the woods. I know something's coming.

"You need to go to Florida," she says. "I won't be the one holding you back."

"Nobody thinks that."

"If you're leaving in three days, we have a lot to do." She shakes the water off the radishes and drops them into a bowl. When she turns around, her lips are pursed. For a minute, when I think of standing on that Florida stage, I can't remember the lines to my poem.

She pulls a long piece of paper from the miscellaneous drawer.

"That's a lot of paper," I tell her.

"Florida's a long way from here. Now what do we need to do?" She writes down calling her sister to take me to the airport because I don't drive in the city anymore, and calling Liz about using taxis and tipping hotel people, and buying traveler's checks and maybe even buying some cooler shirts. She's writing steady, and beads of sweat stand on her forehead.

When she gets to the part about making hotel reservations, I say, "I've done that."

She stares at me. "You did? What about calling Continental?"

"I'm doing that this afternoon. And I can fit Edie Lou's map of Orlando in my money belt."

She lays her pen down and wipes her forehead with the blue handkerchief she's had for years. She looks at me like I'm a stranger, then takes my hand, something she's not done in a long time. "I didn't realize until this minute how much you wanted to go," she says.

"Are you too warm?"

She gets up and takes a nitro. "Just a little fibrillation."

"Will you be all right here by yourself?"

"Of course," she says, but she looks tired. I think of Julia's accident and John Mullins, killed in the woods. Things happen so fast.

That night I don't go to sleep for a long time. I look at Doris's pink housecoat, hanging on the back of the bedroom door—the one I bought her ten Christmases ago. And I can hear her irregular breathing that she's had since her second heart surgery.

When I finally drift off, I dream I'm in the Florida airport. The man on the loud speaker says Doris is having trouble breathing and needs to get to the Portland hospital. But they won't let me on the plane. I run from one person to the next saying, "Doris is having trouble breathing. I have to get back to her." But no one listens. Then someone hands me a phone, but I don't know how to dial and can't remember our number. I finally punch 0, and the invention secretary's haughty voice comes on the line.

"I need to talk to Mrs. Martin," I say. "Doris Martin. She's my wife, and..."

"There's no one listed under that name," she says.

"Doris," I say over and over into the phone. "I have to find Doris."

"I'm here, Leo," Doris says, waking me. "What is it?" She turns on the lamp.

"I must have had a dream," I say and think how awful it would be, flying to Florida and never getting back to Doris and Oregon where everything's green.

"A bad dream?" she says and kisses my forehead.

"I wonder if it's too late to get everything done for Florida this year. I doubt I'd win anyway," I say. "They'll probably choose an ode. Or a poem about Nothing."

"Don't be so sure. I think you've got a good chance. I like it that they never get the log out of the canyon. You don't expect it to end that way."

"Really?" I'm surprised she remembered.

"I've been thinking," she says and lays back on the pillow, then closes her eyes. "Maybe I could stand the plane trip. And if I wasn't up to going to the convention, I could cheer you on from the hotel room. Remember we're not getting any younger."

"I know," I say, seeing the dark circles under her eyes. "Maybe next year. When you're feeling stronger."

"But they've chosen your poem for this year. If we get up early..."

"We'd better not this year," I tell her. "It's all right."

She snuggles against me and we lie still. I feel her sigh and drift off. Then I move to my side of the bed, get out quietly and stretch my back and legs.

Doris rouses. "What are you doing, Leo? It's only a little after five."

She starts to sit up. "Go back to sleep," I tell her and kiss her cheek. "It's early."

Downstairs, I find Edie Lou's letter with the Regency number. I read it again then call the reservation woman to say I'm not coming. She says I need to be sure as there are only two rooms left. When I ask her how hot it is, just out of curiosity, she says "Ninety-five." I know the shirt Liz bought me would have been too warm.

I hang up and stare out at the fog that's lifting. Mist glistens on needles of the noble fir seedling I planted when Liz was born. Now it covers the end of the house.

It's six o'clock by the time I climb into my pickup. When I drive past the Valley Store, the downstairs is dark, but I see a light upstairs where Julia and Bert are getting ready. The store opens at seven, but Julia climbs down those stairs early, checking the books on her paperback exchange shelf. On my way back, I'll stop for coffee.

As I drive by Arlyn's, I see him walking slowly across his field, looking up at the trees. I wave, but he doesn't see me. Maybe he's praying. I'm not much for prayer, though I did ask for a little help during Doris' last heart surgery. But I guess if you have to pray, walking through a field surrounded by firs is as good a place as any.

I drive as close as I can to where Carl saw the strange tree, then make my way on foot into the canyon. I walk along overgrown logging roads, climb over stumps, and zig-zag around windfalls and Scottish Broom. I'm starting to think I've missed it, when it's right in front of me, stretching up two hundred fifty feet, the tumor bulging fifty feet from the top. Its bark is thick and cracked, and it dwarfs the fir and vine maple and chittem around it.

As I stare at it, I know this tree's worth writing a poem about. I'll work on one for next year's contest, and Edie Lou will see that, though it's tucked away clear back here, it's a winner all right.

Renovations

Hank

1980

I don't like leaving her moist and loose. A cow can be unpredictable her first time. But when I try throwing a rope over her neck, she swings her head sideways and bawls. Then she plods toward the creek, swollen for May. "Don't wander off," I yell after her. "If you're further along by supper, you're going in."

On the back porch my old hound lets out a howl. I pat his head and have just tugged off a boot when I hear the phone. I yank at the other boot, but it's stubborn, so I step into the kitchen and tiptoe to the living room. When we redecorated, Maybelle wanted to put a second phone in the kitchen. "It's hard getting from room to room in this big house," she said. It was just after we'd married, and I wondered how many calls she was expecting. I rarely got one and was glad of it.

"Hullo?"

"Hank? Oh Good. I've been trying to reach you." It's Advent Arlyn, something I wouldn't call him in front of Maybelle. He's her cousin.

"Yeah," I say. Who else has such bad timing.

"Maybelle called. She couldn't get hold of you and wanted me to check."

"It's calving time. I've been in the field."

"That's what I told her. She was worried. It doesn't help that she's feeling under the weather. You know, she's more anxious."

My knee aches and I try to sit, but the cord won't reach my recliner. "She was fine yesterday when she called to say she got there. Tired was all."

"Most likely just a flu bug," Arlyn says. "I'm sure she'll be fine. She's in good hands with Lovey. Remember, you're in my prayers. If there's anything I can do…"

"Thanks anyway," I tell him. Arlyn can't get it through his head that I'm not religious.

When I dial Lovey, I'm relieved when Maybelle answers. "Arlyn said you weren't feeling well."

"I shouldn't have mentioned it," she says. Her voice sounds softer than usual, but okay. "The doctor couldn't find…"

"Doctor?"

"You know Lovey. She's a worry wart. A little woozy spell and she rushes me off to emergency."

"Should I come down?"

"With your arthritis? You'd be too stiff to move by the time you drove all the way here." She doesn't mention flying. "A little bed rest and I'll be back to my old self," she says. "Lovey won't know what hit her, right?"

"Yup," I say. "Molly's calf will be waiting for you when you get home."

In the kitchen, I open a can of Alpo and scrape it into Basil's dog dish. "She's just tired from the trip," I tell him when he starts eating. "And from redoing this place." I look around the kitchen and wonder if I should have put my foot down. But when I asked her to marry me, she said she'd fix the place up. "A missionary needs to improve things," she said which gave me pause. I finally said, "As long as you don't try to improve me." She snorted a laugh, Maybelle style. "You can't improve people," she said. "That's God's job. I'll stick to fixing the house."

I rinse the can and start to peel off the paper, but then leave it on. And instead of tossing it in the trash, I set it on the sill. Just this one can—until she returns. Before I married her, my cans lined the sills and counter and formed a pyramid atop the fridge. Del Monte peach cans for seedlings. Santiam green bean cans for grease drippings. Cans of tomatoes for screws. Diamond A Beet cans for 3-penny nails. Cans with big kernels of yellow corn for washers. A can garden of fruits and vegetables, even in winter.

I study the dog food tin, pondering what I might have stored in it. When I pointed out the cans to Maybelle on her first visit, she smiled, then blinked at the bags of cans lining the walls. "Lordy, lordy," she said. "You running a recycling center?"

Basil adjusted to Maybelle quicker than I did. A lifetime of batching it is hard to change. I moved from the bungalow on the edge of the pasture into my folks' house after they died. I never planned to marry, especially a missionary. And a cousin of Arlyn's at that. My father would turn over in his grave. But who could have imagined that at sixty-eight, I'd meet a woman who brought Tahiti into my living room.

Just before dinner, Lovey calls to say she's admitted Maybelle to the hospital. She's developed a fever and has a headache. "No cause for alarm," she says. "Just to be on the safe side." There's no phone in her hospital room but Lovey'll keep me posted.

"What's the doctor say?" I ask her.

"He doesn't think there's anything to worry about. It could be the flu, but she's not a spring chicken. So he thinks it's best to monitor her for a couple days. Run some tests. Maybelle says not to stew and for heavens sake, don't drive down. She'll be fine."

Maybelle must have told Lovey how I feel about flying. People say it's safer than driving. Unless you're on the wrong flight. I can't imagine hanging in space with miles of nothing under me. And what about Molly?

Though Lovey says it's a precaution, I can't get 'hospital' out of my mind. I walk into my library and pull out *A Gordon Pym*, the reason Maybelle's here.

It all started when Irene Jenkins, the Grange Lecturer not known for her political savvy, cornered Maybelle in the valley store. She'd heard Arlyn's cousin, a missionary, was in town and wanted her to give a talk about her travels. The night of the program, Irene gave her a ride to the Grange meeting, as Arlyn, who usually attends, was behind on his Sunday sermon for his congregation of two. Well, three now, with the hippie guy who's moved into one of his two rentals. If Arlyn's hoping to convert his renters, I'm guessing it won't work with Clarence Andrews' family who lives in the other one. Being one step removed from the reservation, I can't imagine they'll be excited about a white man's religion.

Of course, I wouldn't have dreamed I'd marry Maybelle. The day Irene walked into the Grange Hall with this squatty, plain-faced missionary woman, cousin Doris started in: "Who is that? Where did she come from? Why is she here?" I wouldn't have taken notice if it hadn't been for the way Maybelle carried herself. She didn't glide or float but looked people square in the eye without confronting them. Maybe when you've crossed jungles and swamps, walking across a Grange Hall isn't a challenge. I detest message peddlers. But she didn't seem holier than thou.

She set up a projector and with a flick of a switch there was Tahiti in the middle of the valley. She and her late husband traveled there and to Samoa by cargo ship, with her washing dishes and cooking and him lading. In Samoa, Sarah Lutu taught her how to preserve breadfruit. She dived for scallops with Tehau and Felicite LeDuc near Papeete. Names and places fell off her tongue as easy as I say Molly and Basil.

After the slides, Georgiana and Irene said, "Isn't that nice." "My goodness, what interesting places." The only real question was from Doris. "Where to next?" she said.

"I'm waiting for word from headquarters, if you know what I mean," Maybelle said, and Doris nodded, as if she did.

I'm not one for talking but figured I'd never get another chance to clear up a mystery. I waited until Doris and Irene left for the kitchen to lay out refreshments and stayed vigilant in case Doris popped back in. I don't trust her.

She's still telling around the Valley how I was too scared to kiss the Mullins girl that Doris insisted I take to the prom. That girl, as boring as church, talked about girls' dresses and how good we'd look on the dance floor. I nodded, but no amount of coaxing would get me out there. That night, when I dropped her off, she lingered at her front door, grinning and blabbing as I focused on her crooked incisors. I finally said, "It's getting late" and walked to the car. If she thought she could wait me out, she didn't know Hank Hekula.

When I crossed the Grange Hall to talk to Maybelle, she looked at me, waiting, but not the way the vapid Mullins girl waited. So I asked her straight out, "Did you go around the Cape of Good Hope?"

"We sure did," she said. "Have you been there?"

"No, but I've always wondered if Gordon Pym followed a real course."

"Gordon Who?"

"You know, Poe's *Narrative*. The ending where they go into a vortex was fiction, of course, but do you think there was a real Pym, or maybe Poe took that route himself?"

"Are you a professor?"

"What? No. A farmer."

"Lordy, lordy," she said. "I've read 'Fall of the House of Usher' and 'The Raven,' but who is this Gordon Pym?"

"It's better read than told," I said and suggested Arlyn must have a copy. But she shook her head. "He has art and history and religion books but an appalling lack of fiction," she said. And before I knew it, I'd invited her to look at my globe and library.

I only intended to point to the globe and show her the book. But when she saw the library, her mouth dropped open. She stood in the middle of the Persian rug my father ordered, because it resembled ones he'd seen in pictures of great houses in the East, then stared at the inlaid oak ceiling. She stroked the wood of the glassed-in cabinets that protected sets of Twain and Kipling and Shakespeare. Except for *Twelfth Night*. My father loaned it to a cousin who never returned it after which he declared that no book should leave the premises. And none had. Until *Gordon Pym*.

Maybelle proclaimed the room magnificent. I found myself telling her that my father, a carpenter, helped build the school and the Methodist Church over the mountain in Mills Port. At the word, 'church,' she didn't look triumphant. So I didn't feel the need to mention that my father said, "You graduate from grade school and high school and some people, college. But no one ever graduates from church. I won't participate in an organization where no one progresses."

My mother called him a heretic and huffed her disapproval. For several years, she made me go to church where I heard banal sermons and stuffy ministers. But when I turned eleven, my father said I could decide. That was my official church graduation day. I never returned.

After lunch I'm getting settled in my recliner to watch the news when I hear the knock. I squint through the partly open blinds and see Doris and Leo's shiny blue Skylark in the driveway. I sit perfectly still, something Maybelle would never do.

Knock, knock, knock. "Hank? Are you in there, Hank? It's Doris."

I cringe, then lower my legs and stand, a painful process due to what my dad called haying hips. He swore that years of riding tractors and tossing bales in the damp Oregon air rusts your joints. I crack the door open, then step in front of it. Doris is already wedged inside the screen, ready to charge, a casserole in her hands.

Fifteen years ago when I was in the hospital with a crushed leg, she and her cronies paid my house a surprise visit. They hauled out my cans, washed my bedding and clothes, rearranged my drawers and threw away out-of-date jellies and jams in my pantry. When I returned, I asked what the hell she thought she was doing.

"It was for your own good," she said. "So you could recuperate in a clean house." I promised myself I'd never let her into my house again.

Of course, when Maybelle moved in, Doris paid a 'welcome wagon' call. Maybelle invited her in, served her coffee and showed her a sample of the new tile she'd chosen for the kitchen. Doris glanced around, checking out doors leading to adjoining rooms, itching to inspect the place. When the renovations were done, I said "no" to a house warming. There's only so much intrusion a man can survive.

Doris grips the dish with potholders and hugs it to her. "We're so worried about Maybelle," she says. "Have you heard anything more?" News travels too fast.

"Lovey thinks it's the flu," I say. "But they'll run tests to be sure." I don't say she's in the hospital. I don't need calls from half the valley.

"Oh my. Are you going down? Leo will feed your stock if you need him to."

"Maybelle said not to come, that she'd be all right."

"You talked to her?" She acts surprised I can use the phone. "We'll hope for the best. First Mount Saint Helens blows, then this," she says as if there's a connection. "We're here if you need us. I thought you could use a hot meal."

"Thanks." I reach for the casserole, but she shakes her head.

"It's hot; you'll burn yourself. I'll set it in the kitchen."

"Just put it there," I say and point to the wide porch rail. "It'll cool down."

"The porch?" she says, shocked, as if I've said I'm flying to Iran to free the hostages.

"Yes. That'll be fine." She glances quickly to see around me, but I step back and start to close the door.

Before it's completely shut, she mutters, "Social skills of a hermit. I don't know how Maybelle can stand it."

I close the door quickly. "She doesn't know what she's talking about," I tell Basil, who lumbers to the corner and sits. "I let her invite Arlyn in here, didn't I?"

Basil lifts his head then plops on the floor, his head flopping across his feet.

All right, so I resisted at first. Inviting someone *in* for dinner isn't like going *out* to Grange where I can make a quick exit when people irritate the hell out of me.

But Maybelle persisted, said Arlyn was her cousin after all, alone in the world.

"By his own doing," I said, thinking about the wife and two kids he alienated.

"Now, honey," Maybelle said. "That was hard on him. He pleaded with her to stay, but she said she couldn't be married to a minister. Not everyone's cut out for that life." Then she reminded me: if it hadn't been for Arlyn, she wouldn't have met me. So I gave in.

And I tried my best to be cordial. But it was a miserable evening. It wasn't just that Arlyn blessed the food until the potatoes were lukewarm. But when we finally started eating, he cited an article that said St. Helens' explosion was 2500 times more powerful than the bomb dropped on Hiroshima. "The amazing might of God's universe," he said.

"But what devastation," Maybelle said.

Arlyn agreed but said things happened for reasons only God knew, that we were all precious in His sight.

I wonder where God was when precious Roy Jenkins's ship sank in Pearl Harbor leaving Francoise a widow and Darla fatherless, or when the vine maple killed precious John Mullins or when precious Julia's wreck left her addled.

Even Maybelle argued with him. "After bad things happen, we have to make the best of them," she said. "But saying they happen for a reason makes it seem God's responsible for doling out pain. Why are some spared and others not?"

If he'd left it at that, I could have held my tongue. But when he took Maybelle's hand and said, "His eye is always on the sparrow," I couldn't stand it.

"I'm not sure about the sparrow," I said. "But there are too many people for God to watch everyone." I wadded my napkin and dropped it onto my cold potatoes.

He stretched his mouth into a nervous smile and forked out the last spears of asparagus from the serving bowl. "Of course there are problems," he said. "But God..."

"God's not the one having kids," I said. "Most of the trouble in this world is caused by four and a half billion people crowding into a small space. There's too much chaos with haves and have-nots and everybody believing something different. I raise cows to butcher and in India they're sacred. You heap onto that complexity millions of extras and you have one hell of a mess. Scientists have been warning us for years but..."

"Well, you're doing your part for the population, aren't you, honey," Maybelle said and announced it was time for dessert.

That night after he left, Maybelle said she knew he could be a Pollyanna, but he had a good heart and didn't hurt anybody."

All I said was, "There's nothing I hate more than an ignorant optimist." Now with Maybelle in the hospital, I wish I'd kept my mouth shut.

It's late afternoon and sprinkling hard when I cross the barnyard and lower pasture to find Molly. With the rain, I want to get her into the barn one way or another. "Here, Molly, bossy, bossy, bossy," I call, hoping for an answer. But I don't expect frenzied bawling from the creek. I start to run but my legs feel rubbery.

By the time I reach the bank, she's standing tail deep in the water, bawling her head off but won't budge when I call her. I plunge in and wade through water up to my chest till I reach her flank. When I see the afterbirth, I frantically reach under the water. The first couple times I come up empty, but when I try further down current, I feel the calf and yank it out. Perfectly formed but lifeless. I rock the calf gently, trying to revive it. I open its mouth and blow air into its throat. I stroke its face. But it's gone.

"You've never walked into the creek, Molly. Why would you do it now?" I push through the current toward her. She nudges the calf hard several times, then lets out a stream of desperate bellows.

"It's too late," I tell her, make my way to the bank and yell for her to follow. But she won't stop bellowing. It's raining hard now, and I'm drenched. I stretch the calf out on the grass and wade back for Molly. I throw a rope over her head and cinch it tight, to get her attention. "You're coming out of here," I say, but she won't budge.

When I remove the rope, a tiny piece of quartz that's stuck in the strands falls out into my hand. How did it get there? I drop it into my shirt pocket then throw my arm across Molly's neck. She's still bawling but doesn't pull away. "It's my fault, too," I tell her. "If only I'd been here a few minutes sooner."

In the kitchen I drop the quartz into the Alpo can on the sill. If Maybelle were here, I'd show her the quartz and tell her about the calf. She'd look sad but say the poor little thing probably didn't suffer long and that the important thing is I've gotten Molly into the barn. I suppose that's true.

My father said, "They're not pets," and warned me about naming them. "You'll get attached and it'll be hard to butcher them." After he died, I thought I'd name just one. Now they all have names and I can't sell a cow once she's calved. A few years back Doris announced at Grange, "Hank's given a new meaning to putting something out to pasture." She said I was running a bovine retirement village. So what if I am. It's none of her business.

I'm not hungry, but Maybelle would say I need to eat, so I carry in Doris's casserole. I put a small helping in the microwave, which I hadn't thought we needed. Maybelle said, "They're so convenient." I was surprised she'd want luxury when she'd seen so much poverty. But she said, "How is my not having a microwave going to help the Lutu's in Samoa?" She didn't push it, as it's my money. I held out for a month, but for her birthday I bought one. Now we use it every day. She was right, as usual.

As I eat Doris' chicken and noodles, I think about how Maybelle would have told her, "Oh good, your specialty. Bless your heart." Then she would have given her a tour, pointing out the new walls and floors, the drawers lined with flowered shelf paper.

You can't open a cupboard or a drawer that doesn't look like spring—the kitchen shelves, bathroom cabinets, the bedroom drawers. She might have told Doris how she traveled country to country papering dirty tabletops and barrels and crates. A trail of shelf paper across the world.

Their last stop would have been Maybelle's pride and joy, the honey room. Bees made a hive in the roof and their honey dripped down the walls. When I showed her the house, I hadn't been in the room for months. I was shocked to see honey had caked the wallpaper, then dried into a crystalline transparency. The room smelled sweetly musty.

"What the devil is that?" Maybelle said, stepping up to sniff the wall. "Honey?"

For an odd moment, it hit me how strange it was to hear "honey" in this house. My parents never said it. And, though I knew it was silly to think about it, I wondered how it would feel to have someone say it to me.

Though Maybelle did most of the work, I pitched in. In the evenings she took me to whichever room she'd painted or papered or made new curtains for and handed me the shelf paper. I cut and she stuck. After the kitchen, though, she didn't ask me to help with big projects. Maybe she saw I'd reached my limit when she suggested I take my cans to the barn.

"I use them all the time," I told her.

"It'll be hard to retile the kitchen floor with bags sitting everywhere."

"What's wrong with the tile?"

"It's chipped and cracked. It *was* good tile but needs a rest, don't you think?"

She has the darndest way of saying things.

When she asked for help with the floor, I told her I'd never tiled anything. "Nothing to it," she said. So she measured, I cut and she laid the tiles on her hands and knees, humming. And not just church songs. 'When You and I Were Young Maggie,' 'The Old Oaken Bucket.'

It's a big kitchen—fifteen by twenty-five. After two days of measuring and cutting and matching edges, we laid the last tile. My legs were cramping and when she stood, she groaned and said, "Boy I thought we'd never come to the end of this." But then she bent to look at a tile. "Oh no," she said, scrutinizing it. "It's chipped." She measured it, then measured another tile to see how we could replace it without ruining anything.

"It's not noticeable," I told her.

She stared at the mistake. "But I'll know it's there every time I walk in here."

I didn't want to lay another tile. "I read once that Japanese artists purposely flaw their work. You know, chip the glaze or jiggle their brush stroke to acknowledge their imperfection and honor the deity," I said emphasizing 'deity.'

She glanced at me, the tile, then back at me. "You're right," she said. "And I thought *I* was the missionary. If I'm not careful, you'll be taking my job." She kissed my cheek as if it were the most normal thing in the world. Then before I could carry the leftover tiles to the porch, she moved closer and turned, facing away from me. "Could you push there," she said, pointing to the small of her back. I'd never pushed a woman's back. "What helps," she said, "is if you push with one hand while I bend back a little."

I didn't move, so she spun me around. "Like this," she said, dug the heel of her hand into the small of my back while she wrapped her other arm around my waist, pushing and pulling at the same time. She turned around and I lay the heel of my hand against the sore spot, the way she'd done. "Harder," she said. "I won't break."

After dinner, I call Lovey who says Maybelle still has a headache and fever. The medication isn't kicking in as well as they hoped, so they're trying a new one. She'll call if there's a change. She says Maybelle asked about Molly .

"She's okay," I tell her. People don't need bad news in the hospital.

When I hang up, I walk to the living room and sit in Maybelle's rocker, an overstuffed armchair I sat in till she came. She said she never sat in a chair that was sturdy and soft and rocked, too. "It's what sitting in heaven would be like," she said. So I moved to the recliner. Though I haven't liked it as much as the rocker, it's been nice to see someone take such pleasure from a chair.

When I start to rock, there's a clunk where the rocker hits the floor. She mentioned it the day before she left. "We have to fix it," she said. "It'd be a shame for a gem like that to get scratched." I push myself out of the chair and drop to my knees. When I groan, Basil whines. "It's just me," I tell him. Then I inspect the rocker. The pad's worn away on one side so there's nothing to glue. Maybelle would know what kind of material to replace it with. I'll search the barn for a piece of rawhide and fix it before she returns. It'll be a nice surprise.

At ten I tell Basil, "Come on. Time for bed." But he hesitates. When Maybelle moved in, she was afraid she'd trip over him so made him a bed downstairs by the stove. He whined a few nights but didn't fuss after that. "Come on," I say again.

Upstairs, he curls up by the dresser. I crawl into bed and drift off for a few minutes. But then I'm startled awake. At first I think it's Maybelle. Sometimes she talks in her sleep. One night she called out, "Kahau, Kahau, I'm stuck. Help me." I glance across the bed and feel a jolt when she isn't there. What if she calls for me in the hospital? Her pillow's flat, so I wad it double. She always folds it under her head to keep her face away from bugs. As much as she traveled, she was terrified of spiders crawling into her mouth.

Basil moans. "It's all right," I tell him and roll away from the empty spot. I can't imagine Maybelle squeamish. But I guess everyone's afraid of something.

My most scared time was the first night she spent in this house. I hurried to the bedroom while she was brushing her teeth, slipped into my pajamas, crawled into bed and closed my eyes. When I heard her enter the room and walk to the bed, I froze.

"Which side you sleep on?" she said.

"This side, the left."

"I'm an either side person," she said. "Had to be in the jungles. Whichever side of the tent or bed had the least chance of scorpions or mosquitoes was where I slept."

"Look at this," she said, with something in her voice that expected me to open my eyes. I forced them open and saw she was facing the opposite wall and unsnapping her brassiere to expose a five-inch scar, zig zagging vertically under her left shoulder blade.

"Being wedged between a tree branch and jagged drainage tile in a canal can play havoc with you." She stooped to pull a blue flannel nightgown out of a bag. "In some places we were in sleeping bags so there weren't any sides to the beds. Sometimes, we didn't have sleeping bags or beds or cots."

Then without warning she turned toward me and pulled off her brassiere before I could close my eyes. Her breasts fell and spread, wide and flat like women in National Geographic. I felt my face flush and held my breath then let it out slowly so she wouldn't think I was breathing hard for any other reason. I would have closed my eyes except she started telling a story. "Once in Africa we spent the night on branches in the jungle because our bedding washed away when we crossed a river. We lost everything," she said, pulling off her slacks, then tugging the nightgown over her head.

"What did you do?"

"The people fixed us up," she said, climbing into bed. She turned her back, snuggled up to me then took my arm and pulled it across her. I held my breath again.

"That's why you better listen when they tell you where the river floods or which plants give you rash. Otherwise, instead of helping them, they end up rescuing you, and you're twice as much trouble as you're worth." I thought about all the rivers she'd crossed and now here she was, lying next to me.

She sandwiched her cold feet between mine. "You're nice and warm," she said. Then she turned her head, and I knew she was looking over her shoulder at me. "What do you say we just get used to sleeping together first," she said. "There's plenty of time."

"Good idea," I said, and wondered how long I would have to hold my breath.

It isn't yet dawn when I wake to everything quiet. I listen for running water and clanging pans, then remember she's gone. She isn't the quietest person. I didn't think I would miss the clatter. A week after she moved in, I told her, "I'm not used to waking to kitchen noises."

"I could moo if you would like that better," she said.

After a bowl of Doris' soup, I pull on my feeding boots. I'm closing the back door, wondering how Molly made it through the night, when the phone rings.

It's Lovey. She says not to be alarmed, but Maybelle's fever is spiking and she isn't lucid some of the time.

"What do you mean?"

"Saying strange things occasionally, though sleeping most of the time. They've moved her into intensive care, just so they can watch her more closely."

"That doesn't sound like the flu."

She hesitates. "The doctor's running tests for meningitis."

"Does this doctor know what he's doing? The flu's not meningitis."

"He's my doctor and I have faith in him," she says. "I'll call you this evening."

"Should I come down?"

"It's up to you, but there's nothing you can do. It's just a matter of waiting it out. But remember, if anybody's faith will get them through....well, hers is strong."

"Yes, that's true," I say and hang up. I walk back and forth from the kitchen to the living room. I'm just reminding Basil that she's always been healthy which gives her reserves, when I hear someone pull up the driveway.

I spread two blind slats and see Arlyn's blue, rattletrap Volkswagon hippie bus he bought from Terrill a few years ago. Arlyn added "with Jesus" to the "Make love, not war," on the side. For once I'm relieved to see him and step out onto the porch.

He strolls up the driveway. When he nears the porch, I'm struck with how he doesn't look a thing like Maybelle. He's tall with chiseled features, like Michelangelo's Giuliano de'Medici. I can see how his wife found him good-looking, but he's not handsome now. He's aged okay, but all you see walking toward you is someone to avoid. His face has lost its features.

I wonder how people see me—probably not as a strong white-haired man with brown eyes and the biggest library in the valley but as reclusive Hank Hekula who, before Maybelle, lived in a ramshackle house. Maybe Maybelle liked me because she didn't know me as the former before she saw the latter. It's amazing anyone can marry someone they've known for years, after they've lost their features.

Arlyn smiles and is climbing the steps when Basil sticks his nose in Arlyn's hand. "Good old Basil," Arlyn says and scratches him under the chin. When Arlyn straightens, Basil whines and plops down with his head on Arlyn's boot.

"Just stopped by to see how you're...."

"Lovey called," I tell him. "She says Maybelle's having moments of delirium." I lean against the railing.

Arlyn frowns, then shakes his head. "I think you need to get there as quickly as you can," he says. "To be with her and encourage her to fight harder when she rallies. You know, coax her back. There's a special bond between husband and wife."

"I thought you were praying for God to bring her through."

"God can always use help," Arlyn says. "I'll be glad to make plane reservations and drive you to the airport."

I shake my head. "Flying..."

"Driving takes too long. I'll call as soon as I make plans." He walks to his car. "I'll be praying," he says. "I'm sure she'll be all right." But he doesn't sound convinced.

My stomach clenches up. But for some reason, I nod.

In the house I sit in my recliner. I tell Basil it's too much. Being off the ground for seven hundred fifty miles. Doris, snooping around while Leo feeds the stock. And Molly needing shoring up. Plus being in the car with Arlyn for two hours on the way to the airport. But then I think of Maybelle, rallying for a moment, and me, reminding her how much Basil misses her.

Everything's quiet except for Basil, who lets out a long, low whine, then rests his chin on my knee. Just the two of us, like before she came. Without the decorating and the back rubs. Without the humming and stories from all over the world.

The next few hours are a blur. I find my mother's old suitcase and pull six pair of underwear and socks out of the drawer Maybelle designated as mine. I climb into my Grange pants and pull on the new shirt Maybelle bought me. At the last minute I throw in a roll of shelf paper and the tiny piece of quartz.

When Leo comes by, I introduce him to Molly and tell her to be a good girl and get her strength back. I refrain from telling Leo that Doris is banned from the house and keep reminding myself they're doing me a favor.

On the way to the airport, Arlyn tries to start a conversation, but I can't think of anything to say. After a while he's quiet. He isn't as cheerful as usual.

On the plane, I fasten my seat belt and grip the armrests. I close my eyes as the plane taxies onto the runway and picks up speed, rushing faster and faster, like it can't wait to enter thin air. As we lift, leaving my stomach behind, I wonder if this is like entering Pym's vortex. Where does it take you? Maybelle would say to heaven. Or perhaps for her, the vortex collapsed, leaving her half there, half here. The half that's there will be fixing things up, that's for sure.

Even though I'm not a talker, Arlyn might be right, that I can coax her back. If I do, her God will miss her more than he can imagine. He'll have to resort to filling up his space again, maybe with empty cans of beans and tomatoes and corn.

Dog Salmon

Harriet

1981

When Sim walks in with the mail, I'm itching to read him my latest letter to the county boys about how stupid they are. If they don't come to their senses, I've warned them I'll splash their idiocy across the front page of *The Oregonian*.

But Sim looks tired. So I tuck the letter in the ear of the blotter. I'll show him after his mother's funeral. He opens the fridge, then closes it.

"There's a pork chop in the green Tupperware," I tell him. "You can eat without me. I had a late breakfast."

I pick up my black dress from the table. "Somehow I've ripped out this hem—about five inches worth. Before tomorrow, I need to fix…"

"You don't need to go tomorrow," he says, dropping onto the couch.

"What do you mean? Of course I'm going."

He clears his throat. "Well, it's really better if you don't." He pulls a letter from his pocket. "According to the lawyer there's a clause in Mother's will. If you attend the funeral, this place will go to the Red Cross."

"What?"

He hands me the letter. "Why would she do that?" I say.

He sighs. "Maybe because Doris' nephew got fired, and she...well...kind of blamed you for it. And Doris was Mother's best friend."

"I didn't ask for anybody to get fired. But the way that kid was hauling logs over the mountain, he was going to kill somebody."

"I guess it must have hit Mother hard."

"She wasn't in her right mind." I move to the couch. "Look at all we did after Pop died?"

He frowns.

"Well, all *you* did, but I stayed by myself at night for a month so she wouldn't be alone."

He rubs his knuckles against his temple like he does when he's upset.

"After all the years you've farmed this place and taken care of the livestock."

"She was upset when Doris quit talking to her. I should have done something."

"Honey, you can't blame yourself. What could you have said?" I rest my head against his shoulder. I want to say, "You were just letting her poison run off you," but slinging mud at the dead's not right.

"All *I* did was try to make the mountain safer for *all* of us," I tell him. "You know how this valley is. *Someone* has to speak up."

"But does it always have to be you?"

I stare at him. "You can't mean that. All these years, I've thought you were on my side."

"It's not that," he says, shaking his head. "It's just ..."

"Are you going to the funeral?" I ask him. "You know how it'll look if I'm not there."

He stands slowly. "How can I miss my own mother's funeral, Harriet?"

I wake the next morning to the sound of a whistling kettle. I have a headache and wonder why Sim's up so early. I'm always up first and have breakfast going by six. Then I remember the funeral. It hits me that he could try to slip away without talking to me. In our nearly forty years together, we've had our disagreements—mainly over his mother—but we've never tried to avoid each other. I consider staying in bed until after he leaves but think maybe he'll apologize and tell me if I can't go, he'll stay home, too. I wouldn't let him. But it'd mean the world if he offered.

I slip downstairs and tiptoe to the kitchen door. He's in his black suit and dress shoes. His dirty breakfast dishes are stacked on the counter. A plate's set for me at the table, and the oven light's burning. He walks to the kettle and pours water into his cup.

"Morning," I say, and he jerks around.

"I tried to be quiet," he says. "Your breakfast is in the oven."

"Thanks." I take out the tin with toast and scrambled eggs.

He nods, pulls on his coat, then hesitates by the door. "I'll see you this afternoon," he says and turns to go.

"What will you say when people wonder where I am?" I ask him, trying to stay calm.

"Probably that you don't feel well."

"That's a lie."

He turns. "What do you want me to say, Harriet?" He takes a step toward me.

"How about the truth?"

He stops, turns back around and strides out the door, shutting it hard.

I wash the dishes and glare at his dust on the road. "You and your valley can go to hell," I say, jamming the last fork into the silverware holder. Then I wander into the den, sign my letter and slide it into a mailer along with a photo of the bridge under water. My heart's not in it this morning. If we didn't have to drive fifteen miles out of our way in flood time to cross the river at Deep Creek, I'd let this town fight its own damn battles.

I think of drawing up a petition but can't concentrate. In a few minutes, the minister will be rattling off Mother Irene's lovely traits for everyone to cry over. Even the store will be closed for the event. The one I'm banned from. I decide to take a drive to clear my head like I do whenever I'm mad at the valley's do-nothing attitude or I can't stand the thought of another joyless meal with Mother Irene.

When I walk down the driveway toward the pickup, my yellow and red tulips comfort me. My mother loved flowers. After she was diagnosed with liver cancer, I drove to my parents' place and hauled in bark dust, bought azaleas and started a berm, something she always wanted. But she never felt they could afford it. Dad ran the edger in the Linton Mill and she took in ironing and babysat for neighbors' kids, but money was always tight. And unlike Dad who was active in the National Lumber Worker's Union in the thirties, picketing or canvassing or passing around petitions until he died eight years ago, she wasn't one to make waves.

One day, when I was planting her a Rhodie, Dad strolled along the edge of the berm. "I'm glad you're fixing things up for your mother, Harriet," he said. "But I'll have to borrow you for a few days to help campaign for Mahoney. Holman's anti-labor and we need to keep pumping Democrats into the Senate. So I dropped the shovel and hit the road. It was when I was canvassing the valley that I met Sim.

As I drive past Crown Zellerbach's clear-cut mess to see how densely they've replanted, I hear the roar of machinery at the bridge. With Reagan in office, we have idiots from the top down. Even Bert said, "Those county boys wouldn't know bridge clearance if you pinned it to their shirts. Money down the drain." But no one around here will take the bull by the horns. As my father used to say, "Things don't just fall into place. You have to force 'em."

At the bridge, a couple hard hats are leaning on their shovels, talking, and two orange county trucks are parked off to the side. People complain about women gabbing, but when it comes to having conversations about nothing, men are the masters. The few times I've gone to the mill with Sim, I've listened to the truckers:

"George got him a White," one'll say.

The other will mumble. "Yup, heard that up Deep Creek from Preacher Arlyn."

Nod. "Preacher Arlene." Chuckle. Silence.

"Over there giving sermons and pulling out one fir a year." Nod, chuckle, silence.

"Yup." Nod, chuckle, silence.

South of the bridge, a crew's unloading a D-8. I approach the bridge slowly and stop.

It's seventy-five, so I've rolled down the window. "Looks like you're about ready to start the bridge," I yell to Mike Boyd. I know him from our water rights fight three years ago.

He swaggers over. "That's right, Harriet," he says, a sneer on his lips. He probably read the note I wrote the commissioners when they proposed the project, pointing out their stupidity.

"Next week. Just setting up the equipment."

"I hear it'll be twenty feet lower than this one."

He glances at the orange hat to his left, then says, "That's right, Harriet. Despite the letters of a concerned citizen or two."

"Big mistake." I shake my head.

"Come on, Harriet. This old arched style went out with the Hessians."

"I don't know about them," I say. "But this new one'll go out with the first high water."

"Now, Harriet, we just make the bridge, not the specs. But I'm sure the county knows what it's doing. It has Timber's best interest at heart," he says, then waves and walks off.

My dad always said, "When somebody tells you to go along with something because so and so has your best interest at heart, be sure and ask 'whose heart?'" I turn around, backing to within a hair's breadth of a county truck, then drive toward home.

When I glance back, Mike and his gang are laughing and shaking their heads.

As I pass Mother Irene's, I pull over on impulse and drive around back. Everyone's at the funeral, but I'm not taking chances. When I step out of the pickup, I feel uneasy, expecting her to appear on the patio. The house looks bigger from the back. It took Sim a month to paint it. And three weeks to shingle it last summer. A nasty job with its steep pitch and dormers. With him so busy, we worked like dogs, keeping on top of the haying and feeding.

I catch myself checking the windows, a habit I got into whenever we visited, in hopes Pop would look out and wave. After he died, I still checked. I liked that he always gave me a hug and called me, "My Harriet."

I tiptoe to the side door but it's locked. Who would want Irene's precious junk? It'll take Sim months to clear it out. She saved everything, even Pop's and Roy's clothes that were too small for Sim. Our Gracie came too early and lived only three days. But after two miscarriages, I gave all her clothes to Nathan's family. They weren't keeping anybody warm here. I can't see being a martyr to your misery.

I try the patio door near Mother Irene's bedroom, but it's locked. So I step carefully between the yellow Azalea bushes and find a window unlatched. I open it, then crawl through. Once in, I sneak through hers and Pop's floral bedroom, trying to evade the stares of dozens of Kewpie dolls. The woman spent hours arranging those damn things, so they'd sit, just so, on her chest of drawers and every shelf and sill.

I hurry into the living room. It's eerie, knowing she's being lowered into the earth, while I'm in her home. I don't feel right using her recliner so settle into Pop's. Though I hate her for striking her final blow, the place feels strangely lonely.

But from the first time I met her, I knew she was trouble. Sim invited me to dinner in this house where he lived with his folks. Even though Timber was in the middle of nowhere, I couldn't say no. From the moment the big blond Republican Swede looked at me with those green eyes, and said, "You need some help?" then lugged an armload of Mahoney posters into the valley store, I was hooked.

A week later, I crossed this threshold. The temperature was at least eighty-five. When I removed my coat, Sim explained, "It's for Mother's condition." When Mother walked in, she seemed nice enough—a small, round, big-bosomed woman, the kind who bakes cookies for grandkids. She embraced me briefly, then said, "I need your help, Sim," and turned to lead him out of that horrible living room, still engulfed by the busiest field of daisy and marigold and poppy wallpaper you can imagine. I'm not sure why, but I felt so dizzy, I had to sit.

"Oh, my dear," she said, and Sim helped me to a chair.

"Are you all right?" he said, his voice surprisingly gentle for such a giant.

I started fanning myself, and he threw open a window. Mother Irene shivered and gave him a pained glance." Just a few minutes," he said. "She's not used to the heat."

"I'll just finish dinner in here where it's warm," she said and tottered off, to the observer as harmless as a kitten before its eyes open.

During dinner she glanced at me occasionally but mostly worried over her men: "You need more turkey, Pop?" "Now Sim, I know how you like my gravy. I made double the usual amount so you could have plenty."

Pop asked about my family. When I said my mother had been in the critical care unit for two weeks, he said with Sim's soothing voice, "That's a shame. Yes it surely is."

But Mother Irene said, "She's in the hospital? I'm surprised you could join us."

I wanted to say, "She sleeps all the time and usually doesn't know me. They're feeding her intravenously." But it seemed defensive. So I said, "She wanted me to come. She's the most unselfish woman I've ever known."

Irene blinked, then passed Sim more turkey. "Here's more brown meat, extra juicy, don't you think?" And Sim forked a thigh and agreed wholeheartedly.

After dinner, when I offered to help in the kitchen, Pop said they'd do the dishes later, that we could play Parcheesi. "Or what about showing Harriet the dairy?" he said.

"I'll bet a city girl doesn't want to see cows," Mother Irene said. But I assured her that's exactly what I wanted to do. "Come with us, Mama," Pop said. She shook her head and said, "My circulation," which elicited nods from Sim and Pop.

"Well, you rest now, Mama," Pop said.

"I will," she said, and when we returned, she'd cleaned everything so thoroughly, there was no sign we'd eaten.

While Pop was setting up Parcheesi in the kitchen, she beckoned me to follow her to a shelf of photos. I glanced at Sim, but he smiled as if I weren't in danger. She pointed out a man in uniform. "Our son, Roy, who died in Pearl Harbor," she said.

"I didn't know," I said and leaned closer to see this handsome man with brown hair and a much slighter build than Sim's. "I'm so sorry. That must have been terrible."

"Nobody can know what it's like losing a son," she said. "A terrible, unnecessary thing, war." She pulled a handkerchief from the front of her dress and blew her nose.

I agreed and rested my hand on her arm.

Then she smiled at me. "Sim's meant everything to us since then. He's all we've got left," she said. "I'm sure you can understand."

"Yes," I said, lifting my hand from her arm. "Perfectly."

I lean my head back and feel the emptiness. Dust drifts in on rays through the south window. I'm sure it settled on shelves the moment she died, finally safe from her sanitizing.

When I notice the rays lowering, I rise from the chair. On the way out, I glance at photos lining the wall where she led me that first day. Sim and Roy as babies. Sim and Roy as young boys. Sim and Roy as teenagers. Sim and Roy in graduation robes. Roy in his uniform. Sim in overalls and flannel shirt, ready for the fields. No wedding photos of Roy and Francoise or Sim and me. No photo of granddaughter, Darla. Not even a photo of Pop. A wall of sons.

As I walk through the bedroom, it hits me that with Mother Irene's iron grip and Sim's peaceful nature, it's a wonder we got married three years after that first visit. I hesitate by the dresser and stare into the mirror. My hair was brown then, before all this gray turned me drab.

"What are *you* looking at?" I ask Kewpie, balancing cockily atop the mirror. "Life can turn on a dime," I tell her, touch her tummy ever so gently and watch her waiver, then topple slowly, wedging herself, unbecomingly, between the mirror and wall.

I'm balancing the checkbook when Sim comes home. I focus on #9002. One hundred fifty dollar electric bill, the highest in the state. Sim's name appeared on my petition for that battle. We're sixty miles from Bonneville Dam, built to generate cheap power. An outrage.

"Doing the checkbook?" Sim says, his voice tense.

I nod without looking up. "Your dinner's in the oven. I already ate."

"Thanks" he says and doesn't linger. I should have at least looked at him. After all, he's just back from the funeral. The one I was forbidden to attend, I remind myself as I tick off the monthly check to the valley store.

I stay in the den, cleaning out files, until I hear the music for *M*A*S*H* on television. Since its first episode, whichever of us turned it on, reminded the other it was time. I wait.

"*M*A*S*H*," he calls, his voice mechanical.

I switch off the light. Just last week we were cuddling on the couch, eating popcorn, laughing at Hawkeye and Radar. And afterwards, he reached for me in bed. Tonight I want to join him. But when I think how he blamed me for fighting my battles and saying, "Does it always have to be you?" I can't.

I take a deep breath then walk to the living room. "Thanks, but I'm tired," I tell him, surprised he's in his recliner, not waiting for me on the couch.

He glances up, nods, then stares at Hawkeye, who's slicing someone open.

When I walk into our bedroom, I look at the walls covered in navy floral wall paper, Mother Irene's idea. After she gave her 'humble opinion,' she handed a sample to Sim and said, "Don't you like this one?" Then she whispered to me, "You may not know, but Sim's partial to blue." Before I fall asleep, I decide that once the bridge fight's over, I'll strip off the paper and paint the walls pale yellow, a color I'm partial to.

The next day, I rise early, make breakfast then scrub the bathroom. With Irene sick for several weeks, I've neglected cleaning. It'll feel good to tackle something where I can see progress. I start with the tub and after a couple shakes of the can, I'm out of Comet.

When I walk through the living room, Sim's hunched over the desk, paying bills. When he sees me pull on my coat, he looks worried. "Going somewhere?" he asks, trying to sound nonchalant. I know him too well.

"Ran out of Comet," I say. I don't mention mailing my letter.

"I have to shovel out the barn," he says. "I could run by the store."

"It's okay. But thanks anyway."

"I don't mind," he says, closing his ledgers.

"It'll be nice to get out. I'm hungry for vegetables. I'll buy broccoli for dinner."

He forces a smile. He's probably afraid that when I drive by the bridge, I'll get riled up and ask him to sign a petition. He'll never have to worry about that again.

At the bridge they've dug down ten feet, starting the new bridge's approach. Men are standing around, gabbing. If anyone waves, I don't see him. I look the other way and clatter over the bridge. My dad used to say, "Once the lines are drawn, it's best to avoid the enemy."

As I drive past Dunlop's field, I check out their scrawny goats staked out in the weeds by the road. Everyone knows the Dunlop clan has socked away plenty from logging, but they have the poorest animals around. Last spring their cattle grew so thin after eating their grass down to nothing that people talked. Dunlops finally rented pasture from Leo for the herd, but it's obvious their goats are still doing poorly.

Ahead of me, one little black and white kid is stretching, stretching to reach a clump of grass. When I draw parallel to the little guy, he strains so hard, the stake pulls loose. I whip over to the shoulder and stop. I sit a moment, watching him gobble the weeds, then climb out, grab a mallet from the back of the pickup and make my way toward him. "Here, little Strainer," I say, keeping my voice calm. I don't want him to bolt in front of a load of logs.

"What's going on?" I take hold of his rope then scratch his neck until he lifts his head. I keep scratching until he steps forward to smell my hand. He rubs his head against my leg while I drive his stake into the ground and hope it'll hold. The other goats pull against their tethers, making goat noises. "Maa, back at you," I tell them.

When I walk to the pickup, Strainer maa-s until he sees I'm returning with an armload of hay. I toss a leaf in front of each of them and watch them dive in. "Eat up, boys," I say and give Strainer an extra scratch behind the ears. He maa-s loud, then buries his face in the hay again. Dunlops have no business raising animals. A year ago I told them their cows were a disgrace. A few days later they rented Leo's pasture, but now they snub me.

At the store, Julia looks up from her romance novel and nods when I walk in. I drop my letter in the mail. Then I pass the 'This Household Supported by Timber Dollars' tee-shirts and stop at the vegetable bin. There's one bunch of broccoli, but it's turning yellow. Bert walks by without a word.

"This the only broccoli you have?" I ask him.

"That's it. United Grocers' truck comes tomorrow."

"Doesn't look too fresh," I hold it up for him to see.

"Truck'll be here tomorrow."

Just then the front door creaks open and in walks Arlyn, one of the few people I wouldn't mind being shunned by.

"Nice to see you," he says to Bert who grunts and shuffles toward the post office.

"How are you, Julia?" Arlyn says as he passes the cash register where she's perched.

"A good book," she says and I glance toward the counter where she's holding it up. He stops and tips it to look at the jacket. "I've been reading the Good Book myself," he says and grins at her.

"Uh huh," she says and goes back to reading.

I hear Bert chuckle and the thunk, thunk of Sears catalogs being shoved into boxes. Arlyn is making his way toward the post office.

I continue examining the limp broccoli, trying to make up my mind, when I sense someone beside me. "How are you, Harriet?" Arlyn says.

I nod, then look back at the vegetables.

"I didn't see you at the funeral, I wanted to offer my condolences." The Sears thunking stops.

"Um hm. Thanks."

"Sim said you were down with the flu."

There's fake shuffling of mail from the post office. Bert's a nosy bastard. What kind of flu's so bad you can't attend your mother-in-law's funeral but mild enough you recover in a day?

My face feels hot, and I study Arlyn. Is he nosy or just being nice? His eyes are baby doe innocent. In one sentence I can expose Irene for the nasty woman she was. Arlyn's still looking at me, smiling. A man who spends his life waiting for God to instruct him isn't in a hurry. Now, even the fake shuffling in the post office has stopped.

"Well, ..." With Bert listening, the news would beat me home. "Irene ..." And everyone would know Sim lied, despite how it made me look. "I just wasn't able to make it," I say and drop the broccoli back in the bin. "Not that it's anybody's business."

Arlyn flushes. "I was just worried that..."

"Well you and everyone else can stop worrying," I tell him, then head for the door and holler to Bert, who has started chucking Sears into the boxes again, "You should be ashamed of yourself for selling that rotten broccoli."

On the way home, I don't slow at the bridge. Two county slackers, taking a cigarette break, step back quickly from the edge of the road. The dust billows in, and when I start to choke on it, I crank up my window.

Sim's tugging on his field boots when I march through the door. I slam it and glare at him. "I found out why you didn't want me to go to the store."

"I don't know..."

"You don't know that people are asking if I'm sick? You lied."

"To protect you," he says, edging toward the door.

"Yourself is more like it," I say, shaking my finger. "Always avoiding trouble. Lying to me, pretending to support my battles when you don't really believe in them."

His hand drops from the knob and he faces me square on. He shakes his head. "I passed around a couple of your petitions even though some people didn't like it."

"At least they didn't snub *you.*"

"I had to watch them snub *you.*"

"And that was a problem?"

"When you love somebody, you don't want to see them hurt," he says.

"Like your mother?"

"I was talking about you," he says, rubbing his forehead.

"Well you didn't stick by me when it counted," I tell him. "You protected her at the funeral and hung me out to dry. She always gets her way."

He stops rubbing his head and stares at me, his jaw tight as Hank Hekula's bank account. "I married you, didn't I?" he says.

"And after that?"

He shrugs. "A lot of times I didn't accept invitations for us to go to Mother's for dinner because I knew you didn't like to be around her. And I never took her up on her offers to eat with them when I stopped there on my way home."

"She invited you for dinner, knowing I was cooking for you at home? Can't you see how manipulative that is? She's always been in a tug-of-war with me over you."

He looks at his boots a moment, then raises his head. "She wasn't the same after Roy died," he says. "She got scared and clung tight to Pop and me." He makes a move toward the door, but I step closer to him.

"There's no excuse for her disowning us, no matter how you defend her."

He stops and looks at me. "I've defended you all these years. Stuck by you no matter what," he says, his voice icy calm.

"How?"

"Well, let's just say I have and let it go at that."

"If you make a statement, you'd better back it up."

He hesitates a moment. "I went to the county meeting to present your petition to shut down the dump on the mountain even after Hank quit speaking to me because of it."

"Oh for heaven's sake," I tell him. "That dump was a germ-infested eyesore. Besides, Hank doesn't speak to anybody."

"He always spoke to me," he says. "Hank and I were forwards in basketball and ran the 440 relay. He was the only one who ever spent the night at my house. We used to go fishing and camping on Deep Creek. He was my best friend through school and still was—until the dump."

I plop into the nearest chair. "Why didn't you tell me?"

"The damage was done. No sense making you feel bad."

I open my mouth but can't think of a thing to say.

He stands stiff as a pillar, his hand on the knob. Finally he says, "I'd better check the cows. The old Guernsey's off her feed. I'm not sure what's wrong."

"Okay," I tell him but my voice sounds so sheepish, I can hardly hear it.

"I'm sorry," he mutters on his way out.

I nod but don't look at him. I stare into space trying to think what my father would say. But "things don't fall into place; you have to push them," doesn't help.

The next morning I wake at five to find Sim's arm touching mine. In the night, we've wormed our way to the middle of the mattress. His skin's warm. I've always been drawn to the even features and white blond hair of this man I've never fallen out of love with. I lean into him. He doesn't stir. I'm plain as day, but Sim told me after we married, "The first time I saw you, I thought you were the prettiest woman I'd ever seen." That means a lot. And he's repeated that in my Valentine card every year since. I wonder if he still thinks it.

Midmorning I'm in the spare bathroom, stretching masking tape under the sill of the north window. I won't be passing around a bridge petition, so might as well start painting. I hear the door shut and know Sim's back from milking. Then I hear footsteps in the hallway.

"What you doing?" he says, peering around the doorjamb.

"This paint's old," I tell him. "I thought I'd start here then tackle our bedroom."

"That'll be nice," he says.

"What do you think about sage green?"

"Whatever you think." He continues to watch me. Then he says, "Harriet?"

My heart's pounding. "Uh huh?" I say, bracing myself.

"It's the Grange's cleanup day. I wouldn't go, but I promised we could use my winch to pull down the dead tree by the east edge of the Hall."

"That's good," I say, my heart slowing to normal. "It's an accident waiting to happen." I don't offer to go with him. Several years ago, after I passed around a 'no-clear-cutting' petition, Doris Martin walked out of the Hall when I walked in. I've never been back.

"I'll see you later," he says. We usually kiss good-bye, but today we smile and wave.

"I'll fix pork chops and potatoes for dinner," I yell after him.

It's mid-afternoon when I finish the west wall of the bathroom which drinks the paint. It'll take another coat. The breeze through the open window is warm, so I decide to take a walk. I grab a sack on my way out to pick up the trash along the road. Though there isn't much traffic, it's surprising the garbage people scatter around. Especially since the bridge crew invaded the place. It's Sunday, so I walk in silence.

The breeze feels nice and the sun won't set for a couple hours. I pick up two Miller's beer cans and a Twinkies wrapper. I cross to the ditch when I reach Mother Irene's, climb down the bank and find a six-pack carton, baling wire, and a bag of trash. Why aren't people more responsible? I decide I'll pick up both bags on the way back. So I set down my bag and struggle up the bank.

When I reach the bridge, I'm glad to see it still looks intact though they've removed some of the girders. The idiots have dug the road down another five feet to connect with the new bridge. Now, not only the bridge but the road will flood.

On the bridge I step from tie to tie, glimpsing the river below through the three-inch openings. I hesitate at the spot where I took the flood picture and watch the water, now shallow and calm. As I make my way to the other side, I wonder if I was brave or foolish that day to wade onto the bridge planks and snap my shot of the river swirling around my feet.

Maybe sometimes you have to do something, no matter the consequences. Like salmon who butt their heads against the currents just to lay eggs in these creeks. And how do they end up? Rotting on creek banks. Poisoning dogs who eat them.

When I reach the road on the other side of the bridge, I'm ready to go back, when I hear the maa maa of the goats. So I make my way down the long steep incline, the one Sim and I sledded on years ago. We quit after Queen Mother said, "The Baxter's eldest died sledding. It gives me heart palpitations to see you drive off with that sled in your pickup." Why couldn't she tell the truth, that it gave her heart palpitations to see Sim having fun with me?

When the goats see me, they maa in earnest. "Strainer," I yell, then run across the highway. Maa, maa, maa. A chorus. "Where's Strainer?" I say to a gray fellow who's yanking against his rope. I check his stake to see that it's secure. "Now calm down," I tell him, pull a few clumps of grass just beyond his reach and hold them for him to crunch.

"Where's your buddy?" I say again, wander through the troop, then walk further down the road. Is it possible Dunlop's moved some of the poorest goats to better pasture? But just as I'm ready to cross back to the bridge, I spot a black lump on the highway. I run toward it, hoping to find thrown retread. But it's a furry mass.

"Oh Strainer," I say when I reach him. I kneel and touch his fur, matted with blood and dirt. "Why couldn't you stay put, you poor little dickens?" I remove the stake, still hooked to his rope. "Those Dunlops didn't deserve a great little fellow like you." I cradle him in my arms. Then I stand, walk along the shoulder, and turn quickly into the quarter mile paved road leading to their house.

I won't raise a fuss, just hand Strainer to them. As I near the picket fence, I see Dunlop's pickup isn't in the driveway. But I open their wrought-iron gate, step onto their lawn that could stand a mowing, then up onto their porch. I shift Strainer to one arm and knock. No answer. I steal around to the back, listen, then rap louder. My heart's pounding. They're probably at Grange, helping pull out the stump while Strainer's starving.

I circle around to the front porch, pace back and forth a few moments, then stretch Strainer out in their flowered lawn swing and rest his head on the embroidered 'Mother' pillow. It's not like passing around a petition, returning an animal to its owner.

I hear the maa, maa from the road. "I'll be back, little Strainer," I tell him. Through the dusk, I hurry along the driveway, untie one little fellow and the next and the next until I have all ten in tow. Then, reminding myself I'm just watching out for my neighbors, I lead them, maaing and baaing, down the driveway toward greener pastures.

In or Out?

Chet

1982

We have to get out of here. When I stop by Jerry's bedroom to say goodnight, he says, "Grandpa, what kind of glue would stick Lewis and Clark's feet to a box?"

"What you doing, sticking those guys to something?"

"Oregon History project," he says, sitting up in bed, his cowlick pointing to the ceiling. "It's a diorama. The best one gets a prize."

"What about Chief Joseph?"

He shrugs. "Wasn't on the teacher's list," he says, then traces his finger around a fish on his bedspread. "The teacher said Lewis and Clark were explorers," then so soft I can hardly hear, "Mama said Sacagawea was their guide." He stops tracing and looks at me. "Mama said..."

"Better lay down there, Tanas Talapus, my little coyote. It's getting late." I pull the blankets up under his chin.

"What do explorers do, Grandpa?"

"Trespass."

"What's..."

"Go to sleep. You have school tomorrow." I run my hand over his cowlick but it won't stay put. Like his mother.

When I climb into bed, the eerie tree whine seeps into my room, louder than usual. In the moonlight I can see the gold and orange leaves of the maple, waving in front of my narrow window. Small as a squint. At home in The Dalles, I would be sitting in front of my friend Melvin's big-eyed kitchen window, playing poker or gin rummy with him and Gerald. Melvin would be saying, "Chief, you in or out?"

Growing up close to Celilo Falls, we got us jobs at The Dalles sawmill. People left us alone mostly. Just a few "Gonna do the war dance, Chet?" and "wah wahs' when we took time off for the Pendleton Roundup. If I got mad, Melvin said, "Ever see them dance? Look like a couple of mops hanging onto each other."

Gerald didn't say much. When they 'wah-wahed,' he acted like he didn't hear. They 'wah-wahed' louder, then walked off, mumbling how some folks can't take a joke.

"Grandpa?"

"Geeze, a night walker. What you doing?"

"Something's screeching outside. It sounds sad."

"Just the wind, plucking branches. Like a guitar," I tell him. He tugs on a corner of the Tlingit blanket my grandmother gave my mother when she was a girl. The day I moved in, my boy said I'd hauled that thing around so many years, it must be filthy. He hasn't learned what to hang onto.

"Crawl under," I tell Jerry who jumps in, then snuggles against me. He's shaking. "Shiver, shiver, shiver," I say.

"Grandpa? If you're good, do you see people after you die? The ones who died already?"

"Where did you get that?"

"Preacher Arlyn says everybody who's good will end up in heaven together. But how do you know if you're being good?"

"Listen." From far away we hear, "Ahoooo. Ahoooo."

"Our ancestors," I say.

"Huh uh, coyotes," he says. Then "Grandpa?"

"We have to go to sleep."

"Ahoooo. Ahoooo," he says, then giggles.

In the night I wake to rain, pinging on the roof. When my boy Clarence called from here the first week in September, he forgot to say there would be so much rain. All he said in a dog tired voice was, "Dad, if you can't come stay for a while, we'll have to move. I'm working nights and Jerry's going through a lot, losing his mother. Another change would be too hard. Where we live now, rent's cheap. Arlyn, the preacher I rent from, won't charge more if you move in."

"Rent. Rent. Everywhere there's rent," I told him.

"You pay it, too. It's not the reservation. I don't feel like arguing. If you can't come, just tell me." His voice was flat, like when I lost his mother.

That night after the call, I went to Melvin's for cards. "Clarence wants me to live with him for awhile," I said. "Because of Rena's accident."

"Your turn," Melvin said to Gerald, then looked at me. "Let *them* move *here*. You warned him how Rena was. Restless like her father."

"George Rundle," I said.

"George Runaround," Melvin said. "Never stayed at the mill more than a month before he found a better job someplace else. After a couple months, always came back."

We were quiet a minute, waiting for Gerald who stared at his hand like he'd never seen cards. Melvin shook his head. "Too much time," he said, but Gerald didn't budge.

"Any fishing in that place?" Melvin said.

"Clarence says there's trout in a creek that runs behind his house. And lots of fish in the Nehalem River. But you need a license."

"Make you pay to fish?" Melvin said. "That's no good."

"No good fishing here since they buried Celilo," Gerald said, spreading out his cards. "Gin."

"Damn," Melvin said. "No fair. You took too long." He glared at Gerald then scooped up the cards and handed them to me. "Your deal."

I shuffled and thought of the government, saying, "Celilo Falls will be your fishing grounds as long as the sun sets on the Columbia." When they needed to dam up the river, there went the sun. "If I go to Clarence's, I'll get them to move back here as soon as school's out," I said. "And I'm not buying any fishing license."

The letter from Melvin saying they're coming to visit shows up the day Clarence is working a day shift to get the mill ready for the new gang saw.

"New rig costs $15,000," he says that morning, dishing up scrambled eggs.

I tell him, "Should have fixed the old one."

"They're upgrading," he says. "The new one can saw more lumber."

We got a new gang at The Dalles. More lumber through at first, then breakdowns, breakdowns. "Upgrade means upkeep," I say and point to my old black lunch bucket. The metal's worn thin in spots, and it's gray where the paint's chipped. But it held my lunch for years. I found it in Clarence's kitchen, hiding behind a box of canning jars. He's using a shiny blue bucket. "The fasteners still latch good as new," I tell him.

He glances at the bucket but doesn't seem to care it used to be mine.

"Peaches in there. Get you through the day," I say. "Melvin and us picked them. His wife canned them. Best fruit around."

"Uh huh," he says, then walks to the window. "Sky's overcast. Might rain."

"Too much rain. I'm writing Melvin to find us a place in The Dalles."

"What?" He's finally paying attention. "Jerry likes Timber school."

"He wants to be an explorer. He's doing some project about Lewis and Clark."

"With Stephen, the kid next door. He's made friends here."

"He'll make friends in The Dalles."

"It's not just Jerry. I'm feeling at home here," he says then walks to the door.

"Upgrade means break downs." I tell him as he leaves.

After Jerry climbs on the bus, I pull on my jacket. On the porch, I look at the sky. Gray, but no rain yet. Clarence doesn't like me walking around the Valley. He says, "It makes people nervous. They wonder what you're up to." I haven't driven for thirty years and walked everywhere in The Dalles.

I step off the porch and take a detour around the edge of Arlyn's yard to get to the main road so he won't see me. He acts like he needs friends, but I don't like talking in the morning.

When I make my way through the woods by Lydia's place, a yearling jumps across the path, its nose bobbing in the air. I stand still as a rock, watching, but then it starts to rain. I pull my coat around me and head back toward the highway. This place is too wet. In the woods, rain splatters on the maple leaves and bends the fir bows low. In the fields, it splashes on evergreen bushes and Canadian thistles. Next to the creeks it slaps the saw grass down. It runs off the roofs and down the sides of green and white and purple houses. Across the sidewalk from Arlyn's, the hippie house is washed down to bare boards. Sometimes water from puddles splashes halfway up my legs.

Last time I wrote Melvin, I said, "These Tlatskani ancestors didn't die of smallpox. They got soggy and crawled into holes and under rocks to dry out. But when they drained, they were like salmon washed up on creek banks—a heap of brittle bones." Melvin wrote back, "Dear Chief Heap. Get out of there before you disappear. Your poker hand's waiting."

It's pouring by the time I reached the highway, so I take a shortcut by the valley store. I'm almost past the porch, when I hear, "Aren't you cold?" An old woman hobbles out on tall shoes that click when she walks. She pulls a sweater around her. "I'm Georgiana. Come in." Clarence has told me about her.

"I don't need anything."

She cups her hand to her mouth that's painted bright red. "You have a letter," she whispers, like it's a secret.

I've never been in the store, but I want my letter. I step onto the porch and follow Mrs. Clicking Heels through the door. She likes to talk. "We don't see you in here. Just walking down the road. Do you like living at Arlyn's?"

I shrug.

"I heard you don't talk much. Same as my husband. It gets lonely around here."

I follow her to the back of a long room with oiled floorboards and high ceilings. Like in The Dalles before Safeway took over. Except the store at home doesn't have a wall of books that says, 'Julia's Paperback Exchange.'

At the rear, she disappears into the post office. "Here you go," she says, handing me a letter through a square opening in the wall. I see it's Melvin's return address, shove it in my pocket and start toward the front. But she catches up with me. "We're selling raffle tickets for the Pioneer Picnic in May," she says. "It's for a quilt."

I nod but keep walking. I hear a scraping sound, and a voice jumps out beside me. "It's my buffalos. Tickets. Do you want one?" I stop. A ghost-like woman is pushing a stool. Probably the buffalo woman I've heard about.

"It's not *your* ticket, Julia," Mrs. Clicking Heels says. "Everyone's selling them."

I'm not going to a picnic with a bunch of pioneers. I shake my head at Julia who frowns at me, then pushes her way toward her wall of books. I break for the door.

"That's the program where the school kids' projects are judged," Mrs. Clicking Heels says. She tails me and steps with me onto the porch. "I'll bet Jerry has an entry, Mr. Andrews." She touches my arm. "And you can buy a ticket from whoever you want," she whispers, like it's another secret. "You can see Julia's not quite right. Before the accident, she read high-faluting books. I warned my son she wasn't for him. But he didn't pay attention. You can't make them listen. You know?"

"Yup," I say and leave. I don't much like her, but it's true about kids. I warned Clarence that Rena wouldn't stay put. He said, "Don't worry. The Dalles is home." But after they were married a few years and Jerry was six, Rena said a friend told her about mill openings in the Nehalem Valley. They hired women, too. She said, "I'd make a lot more money than at this damned secretarial job."

Clarence didn't want to move. I lived upstairs from them and overheard him say, "Jerry's real close to Dad. They go fishing and Dad's teaching him about the woods."

"It's not as if we'd be thousands of miles away," she said. "We'll visit."

The next day, I told him, "That valley's full of white people."

"Who do you think lives in The Dalles?" he said.

"More of us," I said.

I liked them close, but Rena talked him into leaving. At the mill, she got on clean-up, him on pike pole. One day they needed someone on forklift. She was good with machinery, she said. It turned out, not so good. Her forklift hit a hot wire. Clarence saw the sparks from the pond.

In November Melvin and Gerald come driving up Arlyn's road in an orange Firebird.

I have a roast in the oven and Clarence is sleeping. I've not told him they're coming. He'd say, "How will they get here? Melvin doesn't have a license and Gerald doesn't have a car." If I said that Melvin planned to borrow his boy's car while he was on vacation, Clarence might have tipped the boy off and spoiled everything.

Gerald pulls up to the right house. I'd told them, "Not the big house with the preacher or the dormer house with the hippies." I walk onto the porch. "Surprised you made it in that thing," I say when Gerald climbs out.

"Hey," Melvin says, opening his door but not getting out. He looks old. Gerald walks around to Melvin's door and reaches down to pull him up.

"What's wrong with him?" I say.

"Damn car's so low, can't budge," Melvin says.

Gerald squints. "Got a toilet?"

I point to the house. "Halfway down the hall. On the left. Don't wake my boy."

He nods and carries a bedroll into the house.

"Hey, Grandpa," Jerry yells, running toward Melvin and me. He's just walked up Arlyn's road from the bus.

"Remember Melvin from home?" I say.

"Hey, Qengi maita?" Melvin says, but Jerry frowns, then looks at me.

I bend and whisper in his ear. "How you doing?"

"Who's the kid who doesn't know his language?" Melvin says.

"I'm Tanas Talapus," Jerry tells him.

"Could that be Little Coyote?" Melvin says. Then he grabs him around the head and knuckles his hair. "Yup, it's him, all right. His hair still points to the sky."

Jerry wriggle free and laughs. "How come you're here?"

"To take Chief home," Melvin says and points at me.

"Why you call him that?" Jerry says.

"Don't you know? He's the big boss. You have to do what he says."

Jerry shakes his head and puts his arm through mine. "Grandpa's staying with us."

Gerald steps out onto the porch. "Remember Chief's grandson?" Melvin says.

Gerald nods.

"Cugga mitta," Jerry says.

Everyone laughs. "Pretty close, kid. Catches on fast, yeah?" Melvin says to Gerald, who nods again.

"Talkative ain't he? Couldn't get him to shut up on the road," Melvin says. "Any chance of getting a drink? Heard there's plenty of water around here."

I lead them into the house. Jerry gets Melvin a drink, then takes us to his room. Gerald says Melvin can have Jerry's bed and he'll take the floor. Melvin doesn't argue.

Jerry says, "I get to sleep with Grandpa."

"Yeah," I say. "Jerry Kicken Squirm," then poke him in the ribs.

When Melvin spots Jerry's project, he says, "What you makin'?"

"Lewis and Clark," Jerry says. He lifts the box up for Melvin to see. "They were explorers." He pulls a figurine off the shelf. "And Sacajawea pointed the way."

Melvin takes the figurine and looks at it carefully. "You need a *real* Indian, not Sack-a-potatoes."

Jerry stops smiling and gets that stubborn lip his mother had when she said she wanted to move. But then his lip quivers.

"Good job, though," Melvin says and puts his arm around Jerry. Then he points to Gerald who's rolling out his blanket. "A real Indian right there. See how he gets the wrinkles out from years of sleeping on the ground."

"Really?" Jerry says.

Gerald shakes his head. "Melvin shoot-the-breeze," he says.

"Made you talk," Melvin says.

When Clarence strolls into the kitchen, he stops and stares at us, eating dinner. "Where you guys come from?" He walks to the window. "God damn. You drove Russell's car?"

"You cussed," Jerry says, and we all laugh.

"When you coming home, away from the floods?" Melvin says.

"It's good here," Clarence says, sitting down to eat.

"Stubborn mule," Melvin says, then looks at me. "Catch any fish yet?"

"Waiting for you," I tell him. "No fun by myself."

"You don't know what you're missing," he says to Clarence, then tells about the time he and I were fishing Celilo from a steep rock, and the electric company guy showed up. "He tottered his way up the rocks to say if I didn't pay my bill, they'd turn off the electricity. So I said I didn't use it in the summer anyway. And the guy says, 'Well, Mr. Thompson, you'll have to pay a hook-up fee if we shut it off. You're paying for the privilege to use it later. You need to plan ahead.'"

Melvin grins. "We climbed down leaving 'plan ahead,' clinging. Scared stiff."

"You left him up there?" Clarence says grinning like he hasn't in a while.

"I did, but Chief Do-Good went back and got him," Melvin says.

"Ah," Clarence says. "Not so tough as you let on. A little soft hearted."

"Soft in the head's more like it," Melvin says, stabbing a piece of meat. "All this fishing talk's made me hungry."

It feels good, eating together and talking like old times.

The first week in February it's snowing but no wind. Jerry forgot his lunch, so I walk it to school. The kids are out for recess, bundled up and moving slow. I spot Jerry chasing a kid. He runs up the school steps with Jerry darting after him, three steps at a time. He'd be a good tracker.

I'm cold so pull my coat tighter. Clarence is upset I walk around in the snow. Some guy at the mill told him he shouldn't let his father be outside in this weather.

I told him, "Aren't very sturdy for pioneers, are they."

Stephen, the hippie boy who's off by himself making a snowman, spots me. "Hi Mr. Andrews," he yells. Then "Jerry, your grandpa's here."

"Grandpa," Jerry whoops and runs to the fence. The other kids stop and stare at me, except the hippie kid who keeps working on his snowman. Clarence told me that with my braid, I look like a hippie. "Except their hair's shorter," he said.

"You forgot your lunch," I tell Jerry and hand it over the fence.

He takes it, then pulls off his cap and hands it to me. "You look cold Grandpa."

"Keep it. You'll need it to keep warm. You're fast like a deer. Better than that kid."

He lights up. "I'm the fastest one in Cowboys and Indians," he says. I shake my head but don't ask him which one he is.

The daffodils finally pop out everywhere. I don't think I've ever been so glad for spring to get here. In The Dalles they bloomed two weeks ago.

The first week in May I get a letter from Gerald saying Melvin's in the hospital. Doctors are telling him, "Heart flare up. We should do by-pass surgery." Melvin says, "By-pass is for roads." Gerald says as soon as Melvin gets out, he's going to the Washington side for fresh strawberries. "No matter what we say, he's sure they're better than Oregon's," Gerald says, "It'll be hard keeping him down. It could take both of us."

I write him back "It won't be long now. School's out in two weeks." I don't tell him a mill woman invited Clarence to the Pioneer's picnic, and he's acting excited about going.

I've planted beans and potatoes and lettuce on the west side of Arlyn's garden spot. I've already cooked us some beans. I'm hoeing when Clarence comes home from work. He's been walking lighter the last few weeks. He says the woman at the mill told him "It's time to start life again. Spring's a time for flowers and salary raises."

"She seems to know a lot," I say.

Clarence says, "Dad, the woman has a name. It's Lucille."

"You getting a raise?"

"Lucille has a funny sense of humor. Imagine getting raises when they're still thinking of cutting back."

"Any chance you'll get fired?"

"Lucille says they need us both for equal opportunity."

"If you believe that, you're funnier than she is." I shake the dirt off my pants and walk to the house with Clarence on my tail. I wash my hands and pick up my old blanket and a needle and thread. It's fraying at the edge.

"Times have changed, Dad, You don't see that..."

"When you gonna start thinking right?"

He nods toward the blanket. "Filthy," he says and leaves the room.

The day before the picnic, it's raining hard. Jerry's at Stephen's to "touch up the fort," he tells me on his way out the door. He's getting his hopes up about winning.

I sit at the window, not wanting to go out but I'm restless. I wonder how Melvin's doing.

I could call Gerald, but he doesn't like to talk on the phone.

Clarence walks in, holding up a pair of trousers. "You think these would fit you?" he says. "Yours have holes in them."

"For what?"

"The picnic."

"I'm not going."

He stares at me. Then he tosses the trousers on the chair. "Suit yourself," he says. "But *you're* going to tell your grandson."

The next morning, I hear quick footsteps in the kitchen. Clarence has only slept a few hours, but his steps aren't tired. Jerry's door opens and shuts with a creak at 8:00 and his footsteps stop outside my door.

"Isn't Grandpa up yet?" he says to Clarence.

"We have a lot of time," I hear Clarence say. "We won't be leaving till eleven."

I look up at my squinting window, and through the fir boughs I see an overcast sky that hangs across the panes. I hate getting out of bed. I don't want to tell Jerry I'm not going. But I can't imagine seeing Sacajawea helping Lewis and Clark. Lead them in, invite them to stay, follow their orders, end up paying rent.

I eat breakfast by myself. Clarence is getting ready, and Jerry's at Stephen's for more finishing touches. "How many finishing touches they need on that project?" I ask Clarence when he walks through the kitchen. "They've been working on that thing for months, longer than it took Lewis and Clark to tromp out here."

He shrugs. He's not talking to me.

After breakfast, I go to the garden and am pulling weeds, working my fingers into the soil when I hear "Grandpa?"

I turn and see Jerry's hair is slicked down so his cowlick lays nearly flat. "You sneaking up on your old grandpa again?" He's wearing new trousers and a wolf shirt.

"Look," he says. "Stephen's dad silk screened this shirt."

I nod. "The garden's going to be up soon."

I feel his body stretch across my back, and I stick three fingers in the dirt to steady myself. "You're getting big as a horse."

"You'd better get ready, Grandpa," he says, leaning clear over me and peering into my face, upside down.

I pinch his upside-down nose. "I need to get these weeds out so they won't crowd the vegetables."

He pushes himself off my back and stands up very slowly. "You're not going?" He stares at me, then sets his jaw. "You don't even care if we win."

I reach up to touch his cowlick. "Now...."

"Don't," he says, jerks his head away and stomps out of the garden, trampling beans, carrots and squash as he goes.

A half-hour after everyone leaves, the sky clears, and the air warms up. I go into the house and sit in the rocker near the window. A knock at the door makes me jump. When I see it's Arlyn, I go out on the porch, hoping he won't stay.

"Noticed you didn't go to the picnic," he says. "I was going but don't have my sermon ready. Ideas just aren't flowing. So thought I'd take a walk in the woods, if you want to join me."

"Thanks. But I have to go see Melvin. He's sick."

"One of your friends who came to visit?"

"The one who talked."

"I'll pray for him," he says then looks confused. "But isn't he in The Dalles?"

"Yup," I say, nod, then duck into the house. I don't want to tell him I'm hitchhiking, even though I did it every day when I worked at the mill. The gang-saw man usually picked me up on the way. Clarence asked me, "Why don't you just walk to the guy's house and get a ride?"

I said, "Don't want to bother him."

I shove a pair of long johns and blanket into a knapsack, then tie it around my waist with a thin rope. When I see Arlyn leave, I hurry to the end of his gravel road that hits the highway. It passes the store but the pioneers will have circled their wagons at the picnic. I don't like thinking about Jerry and Clarence. I'll call them from Gerald's. After all, I didn't tell Clarence I would stay forever. He knows I don't like it here.

When I reach the valley store, it looks like the lower dim-lit windows are grinning. The upper porch overhang stares out, mad. Within fifty feet of the place, I see someone moving in short spurts across the porch and down the ramp. I figure it's Julia until I see whoever it is, is moving toward Bert's car. His pickup's gone. I walk slower. I don't want anyone reporting me to Clarence before I hit the highway. But the person spots me and waits. I slow up even more.

"Hey," the woman yells. "Help me. Hey Buffalos," she says.

I don't know what to do. She seems to be swaying. I can't just watch her fall over. "What are you doing?" I say when I reach the 72 Plymouth station wagon.

"I changed my mind and am going to the picnic," she says. She's wearing a heavy black coat and a red scarf on her head. She starts pushing her stool—scrape, scrape—toward the passenger side and hands me the keys as she goes by.

"I'm not going there. Besides, I don't drive," I tell her.

She glares at me. Scrape, scrape—she's heading around to the driver's side.

"Can you drive?" I say.

"I'm not staying Buffalos," she says. "Home."

"Wait," I say and open the passenger door. She scrapes her way there, and I help her in. I lift her stool onto the back seat. The Grange will be a few miles closer to the interstate, and Clarence won't have to know I've driven her until later.

Behind the wheel, I find the brake and signals. I'm glad it's an automatic even though I know I could still shift. But thirty years is a long time to be out of practice.

I turn the key and hold it a little too long. When it screeches, I glance at Julia who frowns and grips the seat. I put the car in drive and pull onto the road where I creep along at twenty-five. Julia doesn't say anything but tightens her grip on the seat when I jerk the car back from the shoulder or brake too soon on the corners.

"There it is," she says when we come to the Grange Hall. It's a big square white building. People are parked on the grass, so I pull off the road and up beside a blue Buick. We bump along for a few feet then jerk to a stop.

"Hey," Julia says, then looks at me, waiting.

"Someone will come out to help you in," I tell her. "I have to go."

"They're all inside. They won't come out," she says and nods toward the steps.

"Just wait a few minutes."

But she isn't waiting. "I don't like it outside," she says and pushes the car door open. I know she can't get her stool out by herself.

"You can't get over the ground. It's too rough."

But she swings her feet out and pushes herself up off the seat.

"All right," I say. "All right." I won't tell Melvin. He'll say, "So the old Buffalo Woman outsmarted you, did she?"

I help her to the top of the stairs, steer her in the direction of the open door and am turning to make my escape when I hear it: "Grandpa? Grandpa?" And then there are footsteps and Jerry runs toward me. "You came, Grandpa," he says, his cheeks flushed. "They're just judging things."

"Julia needed help," I say, but he grabs my hand and smiles at me. Julia's scraping her stool along the floor toward Mrs. Clicking Heels who's waving at me.

"Well, I'll look at your project for a few minutes. But then I'm leaving."

He holds tight to my hand and pulls me into the room, past a table where a woman smiles and holds out a paper and pen to me. "Only five dollars for a membership fee," she says. I shake my head and Jerry weaves me through the crowd. They're wandering around and talking. Some people are eating at the back of the room. I see Clarence, talking to some woman. She's hanging onto a man's arm.

When we make it to the table of projects, an eerie screeching noise comes from the front. An old man they call Pops is playing Red River Valley on his saw and whining out the words. If Melvin heard this, he'd say, "And they think *we* sound funny."

Jerry has hold of my arm and points at the table. There are paintings and animal sculptures and quilts and blankets lined up from one end to the other. Judges are moving along the table, talking about every exhibit. I stand back, watching. I still don't like them doing Lewis and Clark, but I have to admit the kids did a good job.

The saw man's noise scrapes the air. Sawyers at the mill, cutting through spruce, make better music.

"They sure look like explorers," one of the judges is saying. They're leaning over Jerry's and Stephen's box. Jerry's moved down the table where he and Stephen are looking at fossils supposedly found in the Nehalem River.

"This Stephen kid is quite the artist," the judge says.

"Isn't he that hippie kid?" the other one says.

"Well hippie or not, that Indian looks real."

"Who's this Jerry Andrews?" the first one says.

"Isn't he the one whose mother got herself killed in the mill?" the first one says. He reaches into a tin box he's carrying and pulls out a ribbon.

"I don't know. I haven't heard of him," the first one says. "Remember, they have to be from the valley to enter."

"Yeah," the second one says and starts to put the ribbon back in the box.

I step up to the table. "Jerry Andrews is my grandson," I say. "He lives here."

The judge blinks and laughs. "Oh. Well, glad to meet you. These kids are darned good," he says. "Do you live in the Valley? I haven't seen you before."

I nod, step back, then turn and start for the door. I need to get going if I'm going to make the main road before dark. I avoid Julia, who seems like she doesn't know which direction to push her stool. And I don't look at the woman at the "sign up" table. But just before I reach the door, I meet Clarence, coming in.

He frowns. "Where did you come from?"

I shrug. "What you doing outside?"

"Getting some air," he says.

I'm just about to tell him I have to go—I won't say where—when I feel a tug on my arm.

"We only got second," Jerry says, holding up the red ribbon for Clarence and me to see. "Now we won't win the ten dollars."

"Second's really good," Clarence says, but his voice has that hollow sound again. He keeps glancing at Lucille, who's still hanging onto the man's arm. The saw screeches its last note. People hoot and clap and shout. "Another one, Pops," someone says. But the old man bows and hobbles off the stage.

Just then a man pounds on the table. "Ssh, ssh," someone says, and people move toward the chairs. I take a step toward the door, but Jerry grabs my hand and starts moving me in the direction of the chairs. I try to gently pull away, but the buffalo woman pushes her stool in behind me. Before I know it, I'm sitting between Jerry and the buffalo woman. Clarence sits next to Jerry.

"I don't like that saw," the buffalo woman says. "It hurts my ears."

An old man calls the meeting to order then starts the whole thing by having the sign-up woman say a prayer. After that, someone yells, "How about a poem, Leo?"

"After the history," he says. Then Mrs. Clicking Heels stands, holding a paper. I can see her mouth is cherry red from thirty feet. She starts off with a history of the valley, naming all the people who've owned the valley store. I eye the back door. Someone has closed it. Trapped among the pioneers. She talks about how land was cheap, a dollar an acre. Melvin would say, "Real cheap. They stole it from us."

After she talks on and on about the land, she starts listing pioneers who died last year. "Raymond Nordstrom joined the Pioneers in 1910. A member for sixty years. One of the real old timers. And another old timer, Sam Mullins who joined in 1911." She says "It was members like Raymond and Sam who kept our history alive." Who will keep my history alive? Clarence thinks he's a pioneer.

"Rena Andrews," Mrs. Clicking Heels says.

I glance at Clarence who is looking at his shoes. His face is gray.

Jerry lays his head against my shoulder.

"She wasn't a member," she says. "But she did a lot for the valley. She donated baskets to sell when the school needed playground equipment. She took boxes of smoked salmon and homemade jellies to people who couldn't get out at Christmas. And she always volunteered to help with the yearly Grange Hall clean-up. We'll miss her."

I never said she wasn't generous. Two Christmases ago, she made *me* a basket. And the homemade jelly was probably from the same batch she sent me for my birthday.

The buffalo woman is squirming around, leaning into me, fumbling with her coat. Finally she pokes me. "Get this," she says, shaking her elbow toward her scarf. When I pull it out from her collar, she nods toward Jerry. Tears are running down his cheeks. "He misses his mama. He needs to wipe his buffalos," she says. "Eyes."

I hand him the scarf. He pulls it around his neck then blows his nose on one end. I glance at the buffalo woman, but she's still squirming, tugging on her coat.

Jerry uses the other end to dry his eyes. I rub my hand over his cowlick and lean close to his ear. "Those judges made a mistake," I whisper.

He blinks and looks at me.

"Yeah, Chief," I tell him. "You should have won first."

The Accident

1983

Joe

When I walk in, Lydia snaps, "You scared the hell out of me. I've told you a thousand times to knock." She's kneeling on the floor, surrounded by carpet squares.

"Then don't leave your door unlocked." I toss my cap on the couch.

"Just knock," she says, glancing at her watch. "What are you doing here?"

"Carl dropped me off on his way home for lunch. I told him you were out of town, that I was watering your plants."

"I'm sure he bought that."

"He seemed to. What are you making?"

"Laying out the study carpet," she says, arranging colorful blocks on a piece of canvas like a jigsaw puzzle. Her painter's smock with The Virgin Mary on the back has a splash of red over Mary's heart. I know she's silk-screened it herself, but I don't ask what the red is. She'll say something like, "Mary's blood for suffering," and emphasize "Mary." Then she'll remind me that women suffer and men get the credit.

"Nice." I point to her hair, piled on her head in a wad. The ends stick out like cut guy wires. "Do I see a little gray?"

"You won't by tonight. It's bad enough, sleeping with a younger man without being reminded of it whenever I look in the mirror." She taps her finger on my thinning spot. "When yours is gone, I'll let mine go white." She shoves a red block in against a blue one, hard.

"All right, what's eating you?" I pick up a piece of rose applique from a little box and turn it over. It feels nubby. Her place is filled with boxes of beads and cloth and leather. And she insists I call things by their right names. "If I can remember brake shoes and board feet and diesel fuel, the least you can do is call this applique, not a flower thing," she told me a few months after we met. You can't really argue with that.

"I hear there's a new woman at the mill," she says.

"So that's it."

She just looks at me, waiting.

"Not new. Just moved to day shift. Clarence Andrews and his family are moving back to The Dalles. It's his last week. They're shifting people around and adding temps to get us through Christmas. Lucille's been there four, five years." I hand her the orange square she points to.

She nods and exchanges the red for an aqua. "Young I hear."

"Hadn't noticed." Ever since I visited hippie Moonbeam a couple times after Lydia and I first met, she's convinced I'm on the make. She won't believe that nothing went on with Moonbeam even though I've told her all she wanted to do was meditate and talk about herbs. Several months later, Moonbeam turned out to be a lesbian. Seems proof enough.

Lydia says, "I suppose she's about your age."

"Probably, but who cares? This age thing's got you all uptight."

"I never planned on dating someone young enough to be my son," she says. "Being somebody's mother isn't my cup of tea."

I don't remind her she *is* a mother, raising a granddaughter. Her daughter, Jacki, is a sore subject at the best of times.

"Well, I gotta go. Just stopped by," I say and pull on my coat. "I don't have much time, since I'm walking."

She doesn't budge. Driving me back to work would really make the jaws flap. On the way out, I notice empty boxes by the novel/ short fiction genre shelves. I slept through genres in school. But building a woman poetry, essay and novel shelves teaches you more about genres than you can learn in class.

"What you moving these books for?"

"Moving, period," she says.

She's threatened to move before, but hasn't boxed anything up. "Lydie, Lydie."

"You'll think Lydie, Lydie when I'm not around anymore."

I shrug, thinking it's best not to push it. Sometimes dwelling on something makes it harder for a person to back down. "We still on for supper? Remember I'm bringing that venison Carl gave me. Hallie loved the way I fixed it last time."

She acts like she's ignoring me, then gives her head a quick, nervous nod so the hair flops in every direction.

"That a yes or you contacting aliens?" I point to her head, then exit quickly. When I look back through the window, she's shaking her fist at me. But she's grinning.

Lydia

Waltzing in, waltzing out. Free as a breeze. Young women here and there. I turn up the radio and sing *Total Eclipse of the Heart* along with Bonnie while I stack the poetry and sewing books by size on the floor. Joe says I can fit more into a box than any person alive. He helped me move in when I bought this place ten years ago. "You got lead in this box?" he said.

"Cook books and Time-Life books," I said. "And novels wedged in around the sides." When I was married, my husband and I moved every four months. I lived out of boxes until Jacki was born. We were in Idaho at the time. My husband said, "Why don't you stay here while I get settled in Montana." He had a job on a road crew. He'd send money, he said. I waited for the money, which never came. Neither did he. I vowed that I'd never let that happen again.

"You choose impossible relationships, you're going to get burned," my mother told me when I started dating Joe. Of course, she should talk. But she's right about that. Somebody in diapers when you were in your acne stage isn't going to stay put. He's looking, looking. And I'm tired of secrets. We don't go out. Not that I want to. I've become a homebody. But it's the reason we don't go out that bothers me. This place is too small for oddities. Dating a younger man in plain daylight? I don't need that kind of gossip. Especially working at the store.

I've had thoughts of leaving in the past. But now that Hallie's graduating, what's there to stay for? Maybe in another town I can find somebody older. Or nobody. But I'm not going to wait for Joe to move on right under my nose.

Joe

Lydia's right. People talk. If I'm a minute late from lunch at the valley store, guys at the mill say, "Helping the waitress make shakes?" Then they poke each other. Lydia's been working part-time for Julia and Bert for fifteen years, even before she moved to Timber.

Before Georgiana stopped helping at the store, I'd say, "Yup, Georgiana's some gal." They'd guffaw and say, "How is an older woman?"

Sometimes when guys say, "Saw your truck at Lydia's," I tell them, "Yeah parked there and sprinted over to Tarbells to see Barda." That always brings a laugh. Then I shrug and walk off. They don't push it. A couple years ago a new guy on cleanup said, "I've seen the young meat you're after at Lydia's." Before I could think, I stepped up so close to him, he was looking at my Adam's Apple. I told him, "You're better keep your damned mouth shut." It's not only that Hallie is Lydia's granddaughter; she's like my own kid.

When I'm a mile from the mill, Terrill drives by, hauling a load for Arlyn. He pulls over and hollers out the window, "Need a ride?"

"Oh, well sure," I tell him and climb in.

"It's nice today, isn't it? Clear and crisp. Truck break down?"

"Nah. Stopped by Lydia's."

"How is she?" Terrill says, without cracking a smile.

"Getting ready for Hallie's graduation," I say, feeling uneasy about those boxes of books.

"I can't believe she's graduating," Terrill says, downshifts and pulls off onto the mill road. "The kids love it when Hallie babysits. Lydie's a great mom."

"Yup." Terrill knows Lydie is really Halley's Grandmother. But how they're related doesn't matter to him. People said when Sage had Stephen, all the hippies were his Moms and Dads. When everybody left except Terrill's family, some folks called it 'an experiment gone awry.' All that immoral free love and communal living. But as far as I can tell, Terrill isn't the worst for it and has one of the nicest families around.

As soon as Terrill drops me off in the mill yard, Carl motions me over to a stack of piling he's getting ready to move. "New kid on the pond," he says. "Just through the holidays. Boss wants you to work with him."

"Since when is an off-bearer a pond man?"

Carl shrugs. "Ever since what happened to Rena Andrews, I guess. Made the boss gun shy. Afraid somebody else will make a mistake."

When I glance at the pond, the kid's standing on a log, pushing his pike way out against a spruce that's apt to get away from him.

"God damn it," I say to Carl. "What the hell's he doing?"

"Good God," Carl says.

I sprint to the dock. "Hey," I yell at the kid. "Get off the log." But he can't hear me. I spot Terrill, in the process of dumping his load. It's too late to motion to him. Twenty tons of spruce are sliding down the ramp.

I jump into the boat in case I need to rescue the kid who doesn't have any idea how the pond jumps under a load. Sure enough, when it hits, the floater the kid's standing on leaps under him. He hunches down, like a surfer on the crest. His pike is wobbly, the ends bucking like a stallion. I hold my breath while the kid sways one way, then the other. But miraculously, he keeps his balance. He's lucky this time.

Not like that kid a few years ago. And *he* stayed in the boat. But it tipped on him when a load was dumped. He panicked and stepped out, thinking he could walk out on those logs-slippery as glass and unsteady as love. They fished him out, pumped the filth out of him in the nick of time but not before his leg was crushed between a fir and a cedar. He started college and the rest of his life without that leg.

I yell from the boat, "Get the hell off that log." The kid waves like we're having a friendly chat. I pull my boat up close to him and motion him to climb in.

"What the hell you doing?" I ask him.

"Uncle Neal showed me how to separate the spruce from the fir."

"From on top of the logs?"

"From the boat. But I thought I could get closer from up here."

"Get in the damn boat," I say. "You want to end up like the last kid we dug out of here?"

He climbs in. "Huh?"

"A kid lost his leg out here, doing something stupid. You want to end up like that?"

He shakes his head. "I just wanted to do a good job," he says, his face flushing.

He's not a bad kid. "You have to be careful." I tell him. "You staying here long?"

"Just till college starts in January. About a month."

"Well, be careful," I say again, knowing he doesn't have any idea how things happen in a split second. Like Rena Andrews, riding along on the forklift one minute, hitting the cable the next. And me, running toward her, yelling, "Stay where you are," trying to be heard over the mill's grinding and screaming. And her grimacing at me, like she's goofed, then craning her neck upward, trying to figure out where she's caught, all the time climbing toward the ground, toward closing the circuit.

Lydia

At six I hear Joe's knock. He'll follow my orders a few times, then slip into the old routine. He thinks it's stupid that lovers who aren't trying to keep secrets from each other have to be formal. He's told me I can walk in on him anytime I please.

"Come in," I yell. When he opens the door, ducks then steps into the room with fake carefulness, I nod toward the kitchen. "Go to it. I'm going to finish gluing these three squares."

"Joe here?" Hallie yells from the kitchen. "An excuse to quit this damn physics."

"Hey, watch your mouth," Joe tells her. "And keep that book open. How you think those guys launched Challenger? By slacking off on their physics? Now that you've gotten into Pacific, it's the finish that's important, Hal, I'm telling you. The finish."

"Blah, blah," she says, and I know she's covering her ears, showing him she won't listen one more time to his story about making the final point against Rainier and going to the state playoffs. Joe's never had kids, but Hallie's been comfortable with him from the first time he came around, the week after the Mills Port Fourth of July Days where I sold my sculptures.

He told me that day that he'd known women loggers but not sculptors. He came in third, guessing the board feet of lumber in a load. I was amazed by this six-foot-five, two-hundred- forty pound logger being interested in my work. With his whiskers and bulk he looked older, more mature than mid-twenties. I guessed him for maybe thirty-five.

"Seriously," Joe is saying to Hallie. "You need to get a scholarship. Pacific's not cheap."

"Really? You're kidding," Hallie says. "Dibs on the biggest steak."

I tiptoe to the kitchen. Hallie's pointing to the steak she wants.

"Only if you get back to the books," Joe says. The frying pan is on and he's shaking flour on each steak. I suddenly feel sad at this picture that will soon be repainted. For twelve years he's looked familiar in my kitchen.

"The kid's bribing me," he says when I walk in. "There's a head of lettuce in the bag. No tomato. Could you fix the salad?"

"Geeze. Do I have to do everything?" I say and nudge him in the ribs. He winces. I like it that he's ticklish and I'm not. Then he pulls the towel off his shoulder and swats me.

"Would you two quit messing around and hurry up? I'm starving," Hallie says.

At dinner, Joe seems quiet, distracted like he was after his brother John's accident.

"Everything okay at the mill?" I ask him.

"All but this stupid kid who's going to get himself killed."

"What kid?" Hallie asks.

"Sandon's nephew."

"What did he do?" Hallie says.

"He doesn't have brain one, that's all. Standing out on the logs while Terrill's dumping a load. The kid was bucking like a bronco. It really shook Terrill. You know how he loves kids. He apologized all over the place. I told him the kid was going to college in January and that with any luck he'll smarten up. It isn't Terrill's fault the kid's got the brains of a stump."

"Surely you're not the only one keeping an eye on him," I say. "He'll be all right."

"The important thing is, is he cute?" Hallie says. She winks at me and it hits me how much I'm going to miss her. Of course, if I moved, too...

"Good God, no," Joe says. "He's an idiot."

Hallie and I grin at each other then look at Joe, who's trying to keep a straight face. "Is he cute. What kind of a damned question is that?"

Joe

At about nine-thirty Hallie says, "I've got more important things to do than help you two with this dumb carpet. Why don't we just buy one?"

"With what? My store money?" Lydia sounds hurt.

"I know. We have to save for college. Study for a scholarship. Everything's expensive." Hallie hesitates before going to her room. "The carpet looks nice, Lydie," she says. "Really."

Lydie glances at her then sticks out her tongue. "Get outta here."

Hallie salutes and disappears. "Good night rug rats," she hollers. We hear her laughing on the way to her room.

"You've got a great kid there," I whisper to Lydia and kiss her neck.

"Think sweet talking will make me want you to stay?" she says and sits up. "Rub right there, will you?" She points to her left shoulder.

"Sure." I scoop her up.

"Hey, that's not rubbing my back."

"I can rub better in here," I tell her and switch off the light on the way to her bedroom.

"I didn't put the top on the glue," she says. "It'll dry out."

"Glue's not important right now."

"Just let me put the lid on." She's serious.

"Okay, but hurry. My rubbing fingers might get tired."

I hear her rinsing the dishes, putting them in the dishwasher, turning down the heat, making her rounds, the way she always does.

The bedroom's brighter than usual because of a three-quarter moon. The Lalooska totem I brought home from Seattle for her stands in the corner. She's hung an Indian rug on one side and a framed photo of Sitting Bull on the other. We built the frame from Myrtle Wood we found in a Newport mill. In another corner is the oak coat rack I made. Lydia's carved heads of Winnie the Pooh characters hang from the higher limbs. Her flannel shirts and sculpting jackets hang on the lower ones. You can never tell what you'll find in her place since you can never tell what she might come up with. Like giving Barda's mother a bath. No one in her right mind would go over to Barda's, let alone touch her mother. But it's just another project for Lydia. For her, life is a series of shaping and molding and changing.

Oh, she gets sidetracked from time to time, like three years ago when she thought they found Jacki in a ravine in Washington. She lost interest in everything for a couple weeks. But after they determined it wasn't Jacki, that she was still in some dive in Alaska, Lydia started painting a series of canyons. She even had me take her to the ravine near where Carl saw the tree with the bulge. She hiked back up there three times to get the angles in different lights. You can slow her down but you can't stop her.

I've known prettier women, calmer ones, that's for sure. But Lydia wrestles with life, gets every ounce of juice out of it. She won't be pinned. Being with her makes it seem that as long as she's around, life will keep going, no matter what.

The house is finally quiet except for Lydia, moving around the bedroom. She drapes her smock over the coat rack, pulls off her turtleneck and jeans and throws them over the chair, then grabs a baggy tee shirt.

As she crosses to the window, I say, "Don't close the curtains tonight. And what's the point of the tee shirt?"

"You want to get a good look at me in the light?" She's at the window now. "Fat chance," she says, then stops abruptly and takes a slow step back. "Quick, quick. Come here."

"What?" I climb across the bed toward her.

"Ssh. Ssh."

I make my way quietly to the window.

"They're standing right beside my sculpture of them," she whispers. "Grab the camera. It's in that cupboard. I want that."

I kneel by the window, then don't move a muscle. The doe is looking toward me, cautious, while the fawn, with so many spots it's nearly white, feeds close to Lydia's buck.

I feel her hand on my shoulder. "Look at that," she says. "I can't capture that vulnerable shyness, no matter how hard I work at it."

"Maybe it can't be captured."

The pressure of her hand lightens and I know she's going after the camera.

"Don't go," I whisper. "The mother's nervous. You'll miss the whole thing."

She pauses. Then I feel her elbow on my shoulder. She's kneeling. "You're right. The real thing's right here." She leans her head against my shoulder. I wish she didn't mean the deer.

Lydia

"What about Joe?" Hallie says, walking through the garage on her way home from the bus. It's a week before Christmas. I've packed boxes of leather and feathers and am folding a vest I'll use in an Indian wall hanging.

"Is it that time already? Where's the day gone."

"You're dodging my question."

"What about him?" I say, and wonder, if he's so worried, why he just looks at the packed boxes every time he comes over instead of saying something.

"I thought you loved him."

"I do. But I have to think of the future. Joe's going to move on. It's for darned sure I'm not going to have any more kids."

"Does he want kids?"

"Look how he acts around you. And Terrill's kids. Can't you see him throwing a football around with a couple of boys?"

"Have you asked him right out if he wants kids?"

"People don't say what they want. They usually don't even know."

"He's getting kind of old for babies," Hallie says and seems upset. "Aren't I kid enough?"

"Well yes, but...I don't know. It's complicated."

"It doesn't have to be." Hallie opens the door into the house. She's been touchy these last few days.

"It's not happening for a while anyway. I'll stay here until the place sells. Besides, you don't think I could be that far away from you for long, do you?" I yell to her as she steps into the kitchen.

"Maybe I'll stay here and not go to college," she yells back. I listen for the laugh, but it doesn't come.

"Not negotiable," I yell. Good students should go to college. I was a good student and wanted to go, but my parents didn't think a girl needed an education. So as soon as I graduated, I went to work at the Mills Port hardware. I planned to enroll later.

I talked college to my girl, Jacki, from when she was young. And I read to her every day. Get her interested in books, I thought. But when she hit junior high, all she saw was boys. Of course, what did she see when she looked at me? Someone who got pregnant at eighteen and moved in with her parents who helped raise her daughter. Jacki got pregnant at sixteen. Except she left Hallie for me to raise and took off for sights unseen. She didn't come back. It seems to me that each generation leaves sooner. Joe's generation.

Joe

The kid isn't catching on. He's been darned lucky so far, but I don't know how much longer that'll last. The Monday before Christmas, I see him standing at the edge of the raft in the middle of the pond, listening to his Walkman. He has his back to the log dump, and he's reaching out over the water, leaning heavily against the pole. When Carl and Arlyn dump a load and the raft leaps up, the kid comes close to diving into the slime.

When he sees me watching, he waves, takes off his headphones and centers himself on the raft. Last week he told me, "I appreciate your pond tips." Then he gave me a batch of brownies his mother sent to me for keeping an eye on him. He's a real good kid, just doesn't have a lick of sense. It's anybody's guess which will run out first—his luck or December.

While I'm still shaking my head over him, Terrill walks by. "He's a good kid," Terrill says. "A shame he can't clean up around the mill or work anyplace except the pond. He seems hypnotized by the water. Even when he's not poking logs, he's still shoving that pole into the water, measuring how deep the pond is. Or maybe he just likes seeing the pole disappear into the muck. It's like he was a fish in another life." He laughs.

"If he's not careful he'll be food for fish in this one," I tell him.

"Yeah. He doesn't think ahead," Terrill says, as negative a statement as I've heard him make about anybody.

Just then the whistle blows. I glance at the pond immediately.

"He's all right," Terrill says. "You're shutting down for the day. Sandon says the gang has gone through its third set of saws in two hours. No saws left. Last set hit a hazel hoe. I'd better head home." He looks toward his pickup. "I was planning on logging out another couple trees tonight to bring in a little more Christmas money. But Stephen wants me to help him fix his sled. A runner's bent and doesn't go down that hill by Arlyn's fast enough. He's sure it's going to snow. Kids," he says, a big smile on his face.

"Guess I'll go home, too," I say and wave. But at my pick-up, I think how nice it would be not to go home to an empty house. Or to one where someone isn't packing. So I head to the store. Lydia's working until 4:30.

She's cooking turkey burgers for Francoise and another woman when I walk in. Doris Martin is lingering by the ice cream cooler, glancing toward the lunch counter. Lydia's mouth tightens when she sees me, the way it does when she's uneasy. Julia isn't on her stool. Probably taking a nap. She's slowing down but keeps going. I don't know what they'll do without Lydia. Bert rarely comes downstairs these days. But he stays in Timber. Since Georgiana died, there's nothing for him in Seattle.

"The mill shut down," I tell Lydia, nod at Francoise, then sit at the counter next to her friend. "Grill still on?"

Lydia nods and flushes, then pulls hamburger out of the dumpy old refrigerator.

"Busy today?" I ask her, but she mumbles "kind of" as she gives me her 'not now' look. Later, she'll remind me not to come in when she's working. "People can tell we're intimate just by the way we act around each other," she always says. But why all this caution and tiptoeing when she's packing to leave? All this time we've been trying to fool everybody into thinking there isn't anything going on. Maybe the joke's on us.

"Joe?" It's the woman beside me. "Joe Mullins?" She looks familiar. I stare at her a minute. "My god, Darla? I should have known it was you when you were sitting here with your mother." When she turns toward me, I give her a hug. I hear Lydia scraping the grill.

"You want everything on your burger?" she says, her voice crisp.

I nod. "And could you add cheese?" I don't look at her but focus on Darla.

"I thought it was you," Darla says, "but under all those whiskers.... Well, in twenty-some years, we all change."

"You haven't," I tell her. "Except your hair's different."

"And its color," she says. "A lot of gray."

"You went to school together?" Lydia says, acting nonchalant. She moves to the counter.

"Joe got me though algebra," Darla says.

"Then Darla got herself through physics and chemistry and all that other college prep stuff and left the rest of us in the dust. What are you doing these days?"

"I'm home for a month. Between semesters."

"From Japan? Wasn't that where you went after high school?"

"The University of Indiana now," Francoise says. "A professor of political science. I'm very proud of her."

"I'm taking a sabbatical in Bangkok next year, though," Darla says and glances at Francoise. "And Mother's coming to visit."

Francoise fakes a scared face then smiles. "My first time overseas."

"There's no getting out of it," Darla says. "You're coming. Even if Dad decides not to."

Francoise nods, then opens her purse, but Darla shakes her head and hands Lydia the money. "I told you it was on me." She pats her mother's arm. "She never listens to me." Then she puts a three dollar tip on the counter.

"And she doesn't listen to me," Francoise says but is obviously pleased. "Otherwise she would have worn something besides this thin coat. It's cold."

Darla laughs and pulls on a slicker. "Once a mother, always a mother."

"You have family in Indiana?" I ask her.

"An ex-husband but no kids," she says. "You?"

"Neither," I tell her. "You know me."

She nods. "Foot loose and fancy free. Well, who has time for all those complications?" She turns and gives me a hug, then follows her mother to the door.

"Don't stay away so long between visits," I tell her.

"I won't," she says. "It's great to see you."

I wave and turn back toward the counter as they exit. Lydia sets my burger in front of me without saying a word. Her face is bright red.

"You hear that?" I say. "*Darla* thinks it's great to see me."

"There's your chance," she says. "None of those time-consuming complications holding you back. And a professor at that."

"Lydie, Lydie," I say and try to touch her hand as she reaches for the tip. But she pulls it back, without the money. I'm surprised how angry she looks.

Lydia

Two days before Christmas, I'm popping popcorn, getting ready to string the tree. Hallie's at school decorating for the Christmas formal and staying over with a friend. I haven't seen Joe since he came to the store. He called about dinner a couple nights ago, but I said I was busy packing. It's situations like what happened with Darla that make me know it's time to get out. It's not that he's going to follow her to Indiana, but his flirting with someone his own age shows me the inevitable. And Darla's slipping me a three-buck tip for a seven-dollar meal is humiliating. The young professor and the old waitress. I'm sure she couldn't imagine Joe's being with me. I'm surprised Francoise hasn't told her. Maybe we really have convinced the whole Valley that we're just friends.

When the pops slow, I unplug the popper. As I reach for the bowl, a lump of sadness climbs the back of my throat, but I swallow a couple times. Joe's helped decorate the tree ever since we met. I pop; he strings; we both drape. At least next Christmas I won't have to be nostalgic about this one. Knowing I'm getting a jump on warding off next year's sadness, makes the lump slide away. Besides, it's fine being alone.

I've just poured the corn into a bowl when I hear a car in the driveway. And then heavy footsteps and persistent knocking. It sounds like Joe's steps, but no one I knew pounds like that. It startles me. I set down the bowl and walk into the living room, but before I get to the door, Joe opens it and steps in, then slams it hard. His face is red, and he looks upset.

"What are you doing?" I ask him, but he just circles the room, silent.

He pulls a few books out of one of the boxes, glances at the titles, then tosses them back.

"Hey. I had that ready to tape." I arrange the books and close the flaps.

"You're really packing up, huh," he says, still pacing.

"What's the future in staying? Sooner or later, a Darla who's just passing through will return or even stick around. At your invitation."

"Darla? Oh Darla," he says. "I don't care about her."

I sit in the rocker, waiting for him to light. But he continues circling. "It's inevitable. Look at you. Not a gray hair. You think Darla could have imagined you were with me?"

He doesn't seem to hear and wanders over to the tree. "Why do things have to happen at Christmas?" he says and flips a candy cane so that it spirals and catches in the branch above. Then he slumps onto the couch and holds his head in his hands. "God damn it," he says.

"I'll be here till the end of the month."

"What?" he says, like I'm talking Greek.

"Obviously you didn't stop by to talk about my leaving. What's eating you?"

He doesn't answer.

And then I know. "Oh my God, the kid."

He frowns, then shakes his head. "I wish," he says, his voice unsteady.

"What?"

"Terrill..."

"Terrill what?"

"Terrill. God damn it. Terrill. All he wanted was to get a few more bucks for Christmas. They found him under an alder."

"You don't mean...Sage was at the store this afternoon. She's pregnant. Everything was fine. There has to be a mistake."

He shakes his head. "I just keep thinking how he gets up one morning, says good-bye to his family, goes into the woods to do a little logging like he's done hundreds of times. And by the end of the day, he's gone. Just like John." He lays his hands, heavily, against the top of his head, like he's trying to push the idea out.

My heart's pounding, and I can't think of what to say. I know how much he likes Terrill. We all do. I move beside him and put my arm around his shoulder. I can feel his heaviness. "How did it happen?"

He shrugs. "Nobody knows for sure. They think it was one of those splitters, falling in the wrong direction. Arlyn found him. The mules were just standing there, waiting. When he didn't come in for dinner, Sage got worried."

"Two kids and a baby on the way. What'll she do?"

He shakes his head. "I guess Arlyn said he won't charge her rent if she stays."

"Good old Arlyn. This will hit him hard."

Joe stands, paces, then plops down again. "Wouldn't you know it would happen to a guy like him who never hurt anyone. Why couldn't it be an asshole who's not worth a damn?"

I think of my girl, Jacki, who's always stirring up trouble and lives on the edge. "It shouldn't happen to anybody," I tell him. We sit silent for a moment. I think of Jacki and Joe and Hallie, all the people I love. It's hard to breathe and the room is too warm. I feel woozy. When I stand, Joe grabs my arm.

"Don't go," he says.

I sit a moment longer, but I can't breathe. "I'll be back in a minute." I ease my arm out of his grasp and kiss his forehead.

Then I walk into the kitchen, look around and open the door into the garage. The crisp air hitting my cheeks makes me shiver. I spot a box of fabric, not yet taped shut and open it. I slide my hands down, down into the velvets and satins and cottons and watch the ripple of movement as I wiggle my fingers deeper and deeper. The fabric feels soothing. I pull my hands from the box, take deep breaths, then walk back into the kitchen where I pick up the bowl of popcorn and carry it to the living room.

Joe's staring out the window, his forehead resting against the pane. When he glances at me, I see the dark circles under his eyes. "Why do these things happen?" he says.

"I don't know. But do you think you could help me for a minute?" He looks confused but lets me pull him gently to the floor beside me where I give him a needle and thread. Then handing him one fluffy piece of corn after another, I watch him fumble with the needle and fragile kernels but finally manage to make a chain. Then he hangs onto one end and I take the other. "This is too hard to do by myself," I tell him, and we weave the long chain, limb by limb, through the tree.

Goodness and Mercy

Arlyn

1983

The morning of the funeral, I'm wondering how Terrill would feel about Psalms, when the knock startles me. I take another tums, jot 'Rod and Staff' on a pad, and answer the door.

It's Stephen, his eyes dark hollows. "Arlyn, the pipes froze. We forgot to keep the water dripping and Mama and Aunt Olivia don't know what to do," he says.

"Don't worry." My stomach's knotting tighter. "I'll be right there." He nods and I watch him shuffle across the thirty yards of gravel path to his house, his shoulders drooping like an old man's. He's only twelve, thirteen in a couple weeks.

It's three hours later, when I watch them fill the seats of Timber's School Gym. They pull extra chairs from the storage room, stand in the corners, and spill onto the porch. I've never preached to more than three.

I'm uneasy as I scan the group. Sage, hunched in the front row, gazes blankly ahead. Stephen leans against her on one side, Terra on the other. Even with her sister here from Wisconsin, Sage looks too fragile to be carrying one and holding up two. I pray she won't topple.

Murry Tarbell, under the basketball hoop, smiles at everyone who comes through the door. I'm not surprised he's alone. These days, Barda and Carter don't go anywhere. Janice Mullins follows Lanny to the third row where he nods at Sim Jenkins but leaves a seat between himself and Harriet who grimaces, then fixes a sullen glare on me.

There's a cough and rustling of programs. It's time. I take a deep breath and start with "The Lord is my Shepherd," a scripture I've said a hundred times. But before I'm halfway through, my mouth's so dry I can hardly talk. I spot Francoise whose face is pinched from crying, but she tries to smile. Carl hands her a Kleenex.

I swallow and clear my throat. "We're here today to honor Terrill Parker." I talk about how he grew up in Wisconsin, earned a philosophy degree and worked as a carpenter before moving to the Valley. When I say, "He lived by Christ's principles," Sage frowns. "That is, he loved his neighbors and was kind to those who criticized him," I say. Doris Martin squirms on the piano bench.

"Terrill and Sage lived by the old ways," I say, then add, "It's not that we don't have electricity and running water at my place," which brings a ripple of laughter. "But they made most of the things they needed and Terrill logged with mules. They opened their lives to us. They often invited me over for 'share nights' where we told something special that happened that day or read favorite literature passages. They even let me read Bible verses." A few snickers.

"Like the rest of us, Terrill helped his neighbors. He pulled Lanny and Janice out of the snow when they were on their way to the hospital the day the baby was due. He stayed with Jerry Andrews at night for a few weeks after his mother died. Like the rest of us, he picked berries in the summer and worked off and on at the mill. Like the rest of us, he checked the weather and hoped for rain so the woods wouldn't close.

"Like the rest of us he sent his kids to the valley school and signed Harriet's petition against closing it." Harriet sits taller and glances at Sim who gives her a quick smile. "We came to love him because he had a big heart. In fact at 5'6" he was the biggest man I knew." I spot Joe Mullins, drying his eyes. Lydia reaches for his hand.

"Terrill didn't ask that we accept him. He just became one of us while staying true to his ways. God put him in our midst to teach us about love. Let us be assured he rests with God in the nature that he loved." I bow my head. "Surely goodness and mercy shall follow us all the days of our life and we shall dwell in the house of the Lord forever. Amen."

Everyone sits quietly for a moment. Then Sage, Olivia, the kids and I walk out into the December cold. I feel relief but wonder if I talked too long.

With Doris' *Amazing Grace* in the background, people start filing out. I feel a hand on my back and am surprised when Joe Mullins says "Good job, Arlyn." Francoise hugs me briefly and says, "Excellent. I'll see you at prayer service." Carl nods then shakes my hand, the years of setting chokers in his grip. For once, he doesn't avert his gaze but looks straight at me. I relax.

Lydia, who's holding Julia's arm, offers condolences to Sage and smiles at me. I grasp Lanny's hand and Janice says it was a lovely service. Maybelle says in a wobbly voice," You've done yourself proud today, cousin," to which Hank who's steadying her adds, "Yup, not too churchy." High praise.

Leo says, "Appreciated your talk," and pats my back. Harriet shakes Sage's hand and says she's sorry. I'm grateful she doesn't add that anybody who logs alone should have his head examined. Has she gained compassion? Sim shakes my hand and says it's too bad, then walks shyly away. I haven't been touched like this in twenty years.

That night I'm so exhausted, I fall into a deep sleep and wake the next morning feeling like I'm coming down with something. But I remember tonight's prayer service, so push myself out of bed. With yesterday's response, there could be quite a group. As

I scrub the sink, I decide to use Psalms 19:1 as my text, the last thing Terrill said to me Sunday morning before he died.

He'd stopped by early, the way he had every day for the last ten years. He knew I'd be preparing my sermon but said he'd be back in time for church. He was on his way to the woods to pull out an uprooted spruce before it snowed again.

As he exited, a blast of cold air hit me. I shivered, but he lifted his face into it. "The heavens are telling the glory of God; the firmament proclaims his handiwork," he said. Then after a moment, he poked his head back in to tell me not to expect divine help on my sermon. "God will be with me in the woods," he said. "He finds indoors stuffy."

Sage will smile to think of him saying that. And Joe and Lydia, too, if they show up and Carl who, I suppose, will come with Francoise. I can't count on Doris, but Leo did say he appreciated my talk. There'll be Janice and maybe even Lanny who's only come once before.

At five I phone Sage, and Olivia answers. "Just calling to remind Sage that the service is at seven and will be a special one for Terrill," I tell her. "Of course, you're all invited." She hesitates a moment then thanks me.

I set up ten chairs and remove one when, at six, Francoise calls to say she has a cold and doesn't want to infect anyone. She'll see me Sunday.

At six-thirty I hear footsteps on the gravel and look out. Sage, Olivia and the kids are piling into the car. Where are they going? The valley store closes at six. I watch them drive away. Maybe they need air. I throw a couple more logs on the fire. I don't want anyone to be cold. This will be Joe's and Lydia's first time in my home. I jot down a couple more memories I can share, then settle in a chair and wait.

Until seven-thirty. Eight. Eight-thirty. At nine I walk into my study and drop into my chair. My eyes burn; my back aches. How could I have been so foolish as to think anyone would show up? I touch the paperweight Terrill made me from a tree knot and notice my knuckles, veiny and wrinkled.

They've been bending for too many years, picking up and setting down.

I close my eyes. What would Terrill say? That I've done a good job and not to feel bad? That Timber folks appreciate me but just aren't church goers? I try to envision his face, but only see a smashed body under a tree. Suddenly, I feel hopeless and too tired to climb the stairs to bed. So I rest my head on the desk and fall asleep.

When I wake a half hour later, my neck is stiff and my stomach and chest leaden. Am I having a heart attack? I stretch my arms. There aren't shooting pains. I open my Bible to find a comforting verse. I quoted from John 3:16, "For God so loved the world" to Lanny when he was in prison; Isaiah 41:10 "Fear not, for I am with you" for Francoise when Darla went to Japan.

As I flip through the pages, the paper crackles between my fingers, a sound I used to like. Now it grates on me. A fearful feeling rises in me like I had when Bethany and the kids left. I open the middle drawer and search for something to write on. I find an old birthday card from Arnold, my oldest, and scribble on the envelope: "Prepare for Sunday. Paint Stephen's go-cart for his birthday. Show him where Terrill and I logged." I scratch out the last one. It's too soon.

Then I climb the stairs and look into my bedroom. The sheets are pulled up from the bottom. The mattress where Bethany and I slept sags on my side. After she left, I couldn't sleep on it for months.

I open the door to Arnold's old room, pull back the Smokey-the-Bear spread, kick off my shoes and climb in. I'm surprised to see a Daniel Boone cap on the wall. Did he like Daniel Boone? Before she left, Bethany accused me of tuning the family out, replacing them with Christ. "What are you trying to prove?'" she said. I wonder what I told her.

I fall into a fitful sleep. When I wake, I stare at the ceiling, but finally sit on the edge of the bed and do fifteen leg lifts. I probably feel sluggish from lack of exercise. Besides, the air in the house seems stuffy, so I turn down the heat, then walk slowly to the laundry room and find a wrinkled flannel shirt and Levis in the dryer.

As I pull on my pants, I think about Sage and Stephen and feel a sting. It's bad enough that no one else showed up, but *they* knew the service was for Terrill. Is someone sick? Has Sage gone into labor? Though I hope they're all right, if something's happened, it will explain their absence. I decide I'll check on them and after washing up, walk across the path to their house.

Olivia answers the door but doesn't invite me in. Sage sits in the middle of the floor, sorting through baby clothes. Her hair's long and braided like Bethany's. That is until a week before she left. I loved her hair. She said it was in the way and cut it—short.

"Is everything all right?" I say to Olivia.

She shrugs and steps aside so that I can walk around her. I nod to Sage who smiles briefly then says woodenly, "You want a cup of coffee?"

"That sounds good." I relax a little. Sitting with Terrill's family seems like he could walk in any minute and say, "Hey, my friend. How are you?"

But then I notice that Olivia's boxing up books from the shelf. She sees me watching. "I'm trying to convince Sage and the kids to move back to Madison," she says. "We're close to a hospital, and we have plenty of room. We'll find them a place of their own soon. She's in no condition to haul wood, with the baby coming."

"I could get the wood," Stephen says, his eyes swollen.

"I know you can, honey," Sage tells him. "But with a baby, there'll be a lot to do."

His lip quivers. She pats his arm. "I haven't decided yet."

"I'll haul it for you," I tell her. "And don't worry about the rent." Stephen looks at her.

"That's nice of you, Arlyn," she says, her jaw set. "But I need a job. Reagan's trickle-down theory's a nice idea, but it doesn't help if you're up against it."

"It's no problem. If there's anything I can do..."

"I'd appreciate your sorting through Terrill's shed. Even if we stay, I'll need to sell whatever we won't use. I'm sure some of it is yours." Her lip quivers. Terra stumbles out from the bedroom, rubbing her eyes. She flops on the couch and starts pulling at strands of her hair, which results in bald spots. Sage and Terrill have been trying to break her of that, but now Sage doesn't seem to notice.

I look at Terra and try to remember how long it's been since my youngest, Carolyn, was ten. What does she look like now? I wanted to stay in touch but she and Arnold didn't answer my calls and letters. So after many years. I quit trying.

I sip the coffee which burns my lip. I set down the mug. "Well, I'd better be going. I was worried when you didn't come to the service."

Sage glances at Olivia who shakes her head. "Religion's such a personal thing," she says and gives me that forced smile I'm used to seeing on valley people in the store or at the mill when I haul in a load of logs. I force a smile back and tell myself, as I have for forty years: "God, strengthen me at this moment." I wait for a feeling of assurance. But I just feel empty.

I didn't see God as it was rumored. I heard him. While replacing some shingles, I fell from the roof, hit my head against the corner of the house on the way down and was thought dead. While I was out, loving arms reached toward me, pulled me in, made me feel safe. The way you read about. I didn't want to come back. But a voice said, "You have my work to do."

And I woke up.

I wasn't a church goer though my father was devout. But as much as I tried, I couldn't deny it was God's call. It's not something you ask for. You think Christ's disciples wanted to be chosen? To be shunned and mistrusted? Some said the hit on the head made me crazy. Terrill said maybe it was the only way they could explain a man's following a path that cost him his family.

During the time I spent in jail for not paying child support, a therapist told me I'd had a typical near-death experience that could be interpreted in many ways. "Find a steady job," he said. "Then your family will return." I told them Bethany was the steady one, that the few paintings and sculptures I sold hadn't paid the bills. Though I worked in an art shop and even sold vacuum cleaners door to door for a while, before we moved in with my mother here in the valley, we mostly survived on Bethany's teacher's aide salary.

"We're sure you can find some kind of job," he said. After I'd been in jail a month, my mother died and left me the place so I was able to pay my bills. By then, I'd quit trying to explain I wasn't against getting a job. It's just that I already had one.

Late Saturday morning I rise from Arnold's bed where I've slept for several nights. I stare at the coonskin cap, hoping for comfort but feeling despair. I pull a blanket around me and walk downstairs and through the kitchen. I open and shut the refrigerator door, trying to remember when I ate last. Then I weave through the chairs still set up in the living room and into my study where I phone Francoise. As I dial, I cross off, "Prepare Sunday sermon," from my list.

"Francoise?" I say, my voice raspy, as if I haven't talked to anyone for days. I clear my throat. "I must have picked up the bug that you had. I won't be able to have church tomorrow."

"I'm sorry," she says and asks if I want her to send Carl over with chicken soup. She's just made a batch.

"I'll be fine," I tell her and ask her to call Janice. As an afterthought I add "I'm sure I'll be better by Wednesday." I set the phone down with a clank and wonder if I'll find a comforting scripture by then. "Scripture," I say aloud, and it sounds odd. Scripture; Sculpture. Maybe I got a wire crossed.

In the afternoon I pick my way along the icy sidewalk to Terrill's shop. When I step inside, it strikes me how organized he was. Wrenches and pliers and screw drivers and hammers of various sizes hang on nails and hooks along one wall. An anvil rests on a fir chunk we hauled in last summer. Two of his blocks and several lines hang off large hooks on the far wall. Sage will get rid of his logging equipment.

I walk toward the mound in the corner and lift the tarp. It's the go-cart he was making for Stephen's birthday that he showed me two weeks ago. He planned to cover it with a couple coats of black, then wanted me to paint a design on it. "That would mean a lot to Stephen to have a real artist paint it," he said. When I told him my artist days were over, he said, "Don't forget the parable of the talents. You can't hide them."

I'm running my hand across the smooth wood when I hear a noise behind me and drop the tarp.

"What's that, Arlyn?"

"Oh, just a machine."

Stephen steps closer. "Can I see it?"

It's the first time I've seen him curious since the funeral. "You know your birthday's coming up, and your dad..."

"I don't want a birthday this year," he says and takes a step back.

"It probably wasn't for your birthday, just something your dad was making so you could...carry the wood in easier."

He frowns at me as I lift the tarp. "There was too much left to do to have it ready for your birthday," I tell him. "It's not even painted." He inches closer again and bends over the machine, then grips one of the wheels.

"It needs a couple base coats," I say. "What color do you think?"

"I dunno." He sighs and straightens.

"Then maybe you could paint a design or picture on it."

He shakes his head.

"Oh come on. You took second on your project at the Pioneer contest. This could be the best looking go-cart around. Remember God says to use your talents."

"We won't be around anyway," he says, and walks, heavy, out of the shed.

Bethany tried to convince me my talent was painting, not preaching, when I told her about God's call. That first morning I was home from the hospital after my fall, I went to the studio as usual where my easel sat in the east window. Each morning I rose at five and painted the sunrise or colors reflected in the pond. It was my favorite time of day.

At six-thirty each morning I heard Bethany's soft footsteps on the stairs. She didn't want to wake Carolyn who was a light sleeper. In fifteen minutes, Bethany would come into the room with two cups of coffee.

I loved her more at those moments than I was aware of loving her the rest of the day. She was at her softest, her thick black hair falling heavy and uncombed around her face that she'd splashed a little water over, just enough to make her cheeks flush and her eyes bright. I always left my painting for the next thirty minutes, and we sat in wicker chairs watching the sunrise or some days the fog making everything eerie. We often held hands as the rays or fog enveloped the morning.

That first day home, the sun sparkled on the pond and a crane lifted off its surface, trailing its twig legs like streamers. I felt a great calm. Terrill said maybe that's what Wordsworth called a "presence that disturbs me with the joy of elevated thoughts." If that was it, I was in such deep elevated thought that morning that I didn't hear Bethany. She startled me and I felt anxious when she walked into the study.

"Are you all right?" she said, when she saw my blank canvas.

I nodded, and we sat in our chairs as usual. She reached for my hand and waited. Finally, I said, "When I fell, I heard a voice."

"What? What kind of voice?"

"You know, something spiritual, like you hear about."

She was quiet.

"I…well, the voice said 'You have my work to do.' And it felt real."

I could sense her studying me. We'd met at the University of Oregon, fallen in love, then moved to a desert tent community in Arizona which she'd not been eager to leave. But we knew that even though Roosevelt's new Social Security bill might help us later, in the meantime the kids needed more stability. So when my father died, we decided to move to the Valley, knowing we'd be living with my mother.

Bethany took my hand. "You had a terrible fall," she said. "I'm not saying you didn't hear something. But ..." She looked at me. "You almost died. Who knows what might have come to you and what it could mean. The message didn't say 'Christ's work.' There are many religions. I think your *work* means your art."

I could hear the plea in her voice, the desire for us to go on as we'd been doing. It was true the voice hadn't said 'Christianity.' But what else would God call *me* to?

"I just didn't feel like painting this morning is all," I said and kissed her. But I had a feeling of dread. I knew I couldn't let the voice go. I've often thought of that morning and how the moment of change isn't the real moment. It's all the moments before when you're going along like nothing is happening. You feel safe, happy even, your life intact. And all the time you're getting ready to drop off the edge of the world.

Sunday morning there's no smoke rising from Sage's. I feel a heaviness. If she moves, there won't be smoke again. It's barely six when I go to the study, pick up my Bible and read Psalms 20 aloud: "The Lord answer you in the day of trouble!/The name of the God of Jacob protect you!/May he send you help..." I stop. My back aches from cleaning Terrill's shed.

I look at the picture of Jesus hanging above the bookshelf. It strikes me how young he looks. We stare at each other. "I know your life was tragic," I say, "but you had your disciples for company and didn't have to discover what it's like to be old or left behind." I rise from my chair. "Take it from *me*, Lord, at a time like this, rods and staffs don't help at all. No, not one bit," I tell him and leave the room.

Wednesday morning, I call Francoise to tell her I'm canceling services for a few weeks. Taking a break. I tell her I've not had a vacation for a long time and that I'm doing fine. She says she understands. When I hang up, I'm relieved. Then frightened. What will I do with myself?

I pace through the rooms, glancing out the windows. When I see Sage walking toward the house, I open the door before she knocks. She looks frazzled. I ask her in, but she says Terra's sick so she can't stay. She wonders if I'll pick Stephen up from school. She says, "He stayed for basketball practice and with Olivia gone..."

"Of course I'll pick him up," I say. "Olivia left? When the baby comes, I'll be here to..."

"I haven't decided to stay. Olivia flew home to get things ready for us...in case." She shakes her head. "If only we'd left the valley earlier.... Well, Terrill would still be alive."

"That's not up to us to say," I tell her.

"And who is it up to, Arlyn? The good Lord?" Her voice is angry. "When good things happen, we're supposed to give God the credit. And when bad things happen, we're supposed to trust that God has some big plan that's for our benefit but that we're too dumb for him to let us in on. Please don't mention the good Lord to me."

I don't know what to say. I'm in such a habit of defending God, the words just slip out. I think of Randy Baker, the inmate who beat me unconscious, but not before I felt his fingers in my crotch. Not before I asked God to move me to a different cell which happened the next week. I credited the prayers. It was probably the beating. Anyone would have been moved. But what if I hadn't been? And what if I hadn't been thinking then that any sacrifice was worth serving the Lord? Would I have lost my faith and left God? Would I have talked Bethany into coming back?

"I'll get Stephen," I tell Sage and reach around the door for my coat.

Two days before Stephen's birthday, Sage calls to say she isn't sure how to celebrate it. She says, "When I asked him if he wanted to invite his friends, he said he didn't. Terrill was making him a go-cart, but I don't know if it's finished."

"I don't think Stephen's ready for it anyway," I say and tell her about his reaction to seeing it in the shop.

She's quiet a moment, and when she talks, her voice is shaking. "It's all so hard right now. Why did he leave us?" Her voice breaks and she's crying. "And with the baby coming. Sometimes I wish I could just transport myself to Olivia's and let her take over. But Stephen gets upset every time I mention moving. Yet he's not happy here. You're lucky you have your faith," she says and blows her nose. "Sorry."

"That's okay." I think about inviting them here for his birthday dinner. But what would I fix? I'm eating mostly TV dinners myself and canned fruits and vegetables Sage gave me in the summer. I have a small package of Chinook salmon Francoise brought me from Carl's fishing trip. I'm saving it for something special, I don't know what. But there's not enough for all of us.

"Does Stephen have a favorite dinner you could make?" I ask her. "I have cookies in the freezer that Janice gave me for Christmas. We can have those for dessert. And I'll bring a gift."

She sighs. "Okay," she says. "It'll have to do."

When we hang up, I get Arnold's coonskin cap and put it into a leather pouch I used during my hunting years. Arnold won't miss it. Those days are over.

Two nights later Stephen opens the pouch. He frowns and looks closer, then pulls out the cap. I feel a twinge as he sets it on his head. He feels the tail and smiles.

"That's great, honey," Sage says. "You're like Daniel Boone in the old days."

He tugs the cap on more firmly. "Thank you Arlyn," he says, then sighs. "It'll keep my head warm in case we move to Wisconsin."

About a month after the funeral, I wake in Arnold's bed and wonder why I'm not in my own. I check the wall for his coonskin cap and can't remember where it is. Then it all floods back. As I'm not preparing for services, I no longer go to my study. I can't think of a reason to get up until I remember I've told Sage I'll re-gravel the path. The winter's freezing and thawing have turned it to muck.

When I force myself from bed, I wander through the house, room by room, then end up in the kitchen. I make coffee and eat a slice of unbuttered bread. It's too much trouble to toast it. Terrill often popped two slices in the toaster when he came by. "Time for a break," he'd say.

Then I pull on my coat, and step into the overcast chill of February. Though I've always found it the bleakest month, I've been hopeful that spring's coming. Now, I don't care. On my way to the pickup, I pass Clarence's empty house and think about his father, Chet, wandering the valley. Did he feel like he'd come un-moored? Did the move back to The Dalles anchor him? And what about Clarence? Do some people acquire so many scars that no amount of comfort can ease them?

I climb into my pickup and pull out onto the gravel road that leads to the highway.

What's everyone doing today to pass the time? Francoise is teaching. Doris and Leo may be eating lunch at the Mills Port senior center. Janice is working at the hospital and Lanny's watching the baby at the feed store if Janice's mother isn't with them.

I drive toward the county's gravel pit, wondering if anyone's around to sell me a load.

When I pass the valley store, for some reason I pull in. The thought of running into anybody makes me anxious, but my social security check is due and I have nothing in the fridge. I haven't been beyond the end of my road for a couple weeks.

When I walk in, I spot Harriet. If I'd noticed her pickup outside, I would have kept going. But it's too late.

"How can all these heads of lettuce be the same price when they're different sizes?" she's saying to nobody in particular. "And thirty cents a head? They shipped in from Cyprus?"

Julia looks up from her novel, *Romance Under the Sun,* nods at me, then says to Harriet. "Lydia will tell you. Tomorrow." These days, Bert rarely comes downstairs.

I walk around the counter, getting my bearings. What do I need? Milk? Bread? It's hard to buy food when you've lost your appetite.

"Don't you think thirty cents a head is highway robbery?"

Maybe eggs...

"Arlyn?"

"Oh, hello, Harriet."

"I'm asking *you*," she says. "Don't you think it's a god awful price?"

"I haven't bought lettuce for a while," I tell her.

She puts the lettuce back, then pulls it out again. "I told Sim we'd have Crab Louis for lunch. He really likes it. But this is ridiculous." She bounces the lettuce in her hand, feeling its weight. "It's small," she says. "And I'd need two heads."

I nod and turn to walk away.

"Everybody's noncommittal as usual," she says. She now balances one head in each hand, like she's a vegetable scales of justice. "Nobody fights for anything."

"If it'll make Sim happy..."

"You're missing the point," she snaps.

I shrug and turn toward the dairy case. On the way, I pull a dollar from my pocket. I'll just buy milk today and leave the rest till later.

But Harriet follows me to the dairy case. "Do you know some young punk, flying around a curve on the mountain, nearly ran me off the road this morning? But does anybody do a thing?" She steps closer, planting herself between me and the dairy case.

"Well I'm glad you weren't hurt, Harriet. Luck was with you." Lately I've not been giving God credit for anything.

"How can you be so removed," she says, waving an angry palm across my face.

Suddenly I'm suffocating. "Please don't wave your hand in my face," I tell her, letting go of the dairy case handle and turning toward the front of the store.

Harriet blinks a couple times, then stands, haughty. "Every time you spout off Christian rubbish, you're waving your hand in *my* face," she says. "You feel..."

"You don't know what I feel, Harriet," I say, louder than I expected. "Be glad you have Sim. Some of us aren't so lucky."

"Well," she says. "You made your bed. I guess..."

"I guess I will." I make a move toward the door, and glance at my pick-up which seems miles away. On my way past Julia, I slap my dollar on the counter. "For Harriet's lettuce," I say, fighting back tears I thought dried up years ago.

Julia struggles to her feet, pushes her stool to the counter and reaches for the bill. "Wait; your change," she says, but I don't stop.

"What do you think you're doing?" Harriet says, snatching the dollar and catching me before I can open the door. Her eyes blaze, but she blinks when she sees my face.

"I don't take charity from anybody," she says, but her voice is calmer.

"Sim deserves Crab Louie. You need to take care of each other."

She looks at me a moment, skeptical. Then she says, "You should practice what you preach." She points to my sleeve. "Looks like you could use some taking care of."

I feel under my arm. "A hole?"

She shakes her head. "The whole seam. Maybe that Sage woman can fix you up."

"She's probably moving." I swallow hard.

"Hm," she says and ponders a moment. "Well, I guess if it comes to that, I suppose I have needle and thread."

"Thank you, Harriet." I lift my elbow to look at the seam. "I...I hadn't noticed."

"That's a man for you," she says, then charges out the door.

I look at Julia, who points to my shirt, then the counter. "She forgot her lettuce," she says, nodding toward the two small heads.

"She wouldn't let me help her," I say.

"You were trying," Julia says. "Isn't that what Buffalos do, help people?"

I look at her.

"Preachers," she says. "Well don't they?"

"Well...yes. Well maybe they try to anyway."

"That's not so bad," she says. "Is it?"

I look at her a moment. "I suppose not." Then I hand her the dollar and pick up the heads of lettuce. "I think I just might make myself a Chinook Salmon Louis," I tell her.

"Salmon Louis?" She shakes her head.

As I'm going out the door, she laughs. "Crazy Buffalos," I hear her say. "Just a bunch of crazy Buffalos."

Made in USA - North Chelmsford, MA
1216908_9781683150220
12.22.2020 1637